The Duchess Who Dared

CHARLES CASTLE

Swift

SWIFT PRESS

This edition published by Swift Press, 2021
First published in Great Britain by Sidgwick & Jackson, 1994

1 3 5 7 9 10 8 6 4 2

Typeset by Tetragon, London
Printed in England by CPI Group (UK) Ltd, Croydon, CRO 4YY

A CIP catalogue record for this book is available from the British Library

ISBN: 9781800750791
eISBN: 9781800750807

CONTENTS

FOREWORD

MARGARET Whigham, Scots-born socialite and heiress, was an enchantress, considered one of the most beautiful women of her generation and one of the ten best-dressed in the world. Charming, elegant and gregarious, she was as sought after, reported and photographed in the press as a Hollywood film star. Much travelled, she revolutionized the public's previous perception of débutantes in the thirties and took London by storm – then and for many years to come. There seemed few in the political, social, theatrical or movie worlds who either did not know her or who did not wish to make her acquaintance. Some to their detriment.

Her first marriage to the American businessman and golfer Charles Sweeny ended in divorce, but the match produced two children: their daughter became Duchess of Rutland shortly after coming out, and their son a businessman in investments, like his father.

Although Margaret's second marriage, to the Duke of Argyll, lasted only ten years, her divorce from him was the longest, costliest and most scandalous in British divorce history. She paid a phenomenal price when the Duke finally won his freedom. She was also involved in at least seven legal actions running concurrently concerning poison-pen letters, a paternity suit (in which she was threatened with contempt and possible imprisonment), and others relating to libel and slander.

Margaret, Duchess of Argyll, asked me to write her life story over twenty years ago. We first met at the home in New York of our mutual American lawyer Arnold Weissberger during a party to celebrate the publication of my biography *Noël*, based on my television film about the life of Sir Noël Coward. A few months later Margaret telephoned me: she had read my book and was also impressed with the television documentary I had made on the departure of the Duke and Duchess of Bedford from Woburn Abbey. I agreed to her idea on condition that on each occasion we met I could bring a tape recorder to achieve a verbatim account of her story and so that I could report her speech patterns and expressions accurately. Also I needed both copyright and legal protection against any unforeseeable litigation – I was all too aware that her past had been bound up with treachery, adultery and deceit.

I arrived for dinner one evening in 1974 at her Queen Anne house, 48 Upper Grosvenor Street, opposite the American embassy in London's Mayfair. The drawing room, where Margaret was waiting for me, and library were products of the design of Mrs Somerset (Syrie) Maugham, who made popular the 'white on white' décor that became fashionable for salons in London, Paris and New York. Margaret stood at the end of the room, her face to the light, conscious of the effect her appearance would have on me. She had large expressive green eyes and dark auburn hair swept up from her face, arranged daily by the Mayfair society hairdresser Renée. Her carefully applied make-up was immaculate, touched up constantly during dinner and conversation. She had the fine pure white porcelain skin of a woman who had never been exposed to the sun or sullied by liquor: she hardly drank except, perhaps, for a glass of wine at dinner. Her lips were painted bright red, reminding me of the make-up of the thirties when she was at the height of her beauty, and matched perfectly the varnish on the immaculately manicured nails that tipped long, tapered fingers on hands that had never done a day's work. Lean shapely legs, fine ankles and delicate size-three feet were enhanced by smoky grey silk stockings, and her elegant black satin shoes were decorated with diamanté clips. She wore a black silk dress with dark chiffon covering her chest and long, slender arms. Three rows of perfectly matched pearls adorned her neck, fastened with a diamond clasp.

Her staff consisted of a butler, who opened the street door to those courageous enough to venture inside and waited at table with royal aplomb although he was seldom sober, and a maid who was rarely visible since her time was spent in her mistress's boudoir tending exquisite garments by Molyneux and Hartnell and custom-made silk underwear. The cook, Mrs Duckworth, produced simple but good English fare in tiny portions, at which Margaret would pick indifferently. Margaret could boil neither an egg nor water and had never made her own bed.

I followed Margaret into the panelled library across the first-floor landing, and became impressed by her upright stature and her lengthy assertive strides. She reminded me of a quality thoroughbred I had seen at Tattersalls. The two poodles, Marcel and Alphonse, were close at her heels then and were always with her during my visits. We sat opposite one another in low, upholstered chairs on either side of the small elegant sofa on which the poodles pounced. I noticed two electric push-buttons set into the wall within easy reach of her right hand. The small household one summoned the butler, who appeared equipped with the dogs' bowls on a salver. The larger button was connected with the West End police station as well as Fleet Street; she was anxious about protection, having had burglaries and strings of unwanted callers in the past – many of them bearing writs – and, as a rich woman living alone, she was aware of the publicity that any intruder or assailant might bring. Her dependency on such stringent security measures was strangely discomforting and I often found myself staring at the close proximity of her right hand to the buttons.

She was poised and her voice had a soft, sexy, mellifluous timbre, the Mayfair vowels betraying none of her Scottish or American background. She also spoke with a pronounced stammer. As a child she had been sent to speech therapists, who discovered that the reason for this was psychological, due to nervousness caused by insecurity. Throughout our meetings, however, she stammered little: our exchanges were relaxed and friendly.

On my first call she gave a brief summary of her life's pattern and later went into finer detail, illustrating and substantiating her stories with a collection of scrapbooks, immaculately kept in a large cupboard behind her chair. She had a copy of every news-cutting about her chequered life, sent from all corners of the globe. Each volume was bound in bright red leather, and on the gold-engraved spine was the letter 'M' with a coronet above it. Asked why she kept this library of her life so intact she explained that it was for the benefit of her grandchildren: she wanted them to know the truth about her past. I noticed, however, that certain cuttings were missing concerning the Duke of Argyll's children from his former marriage. They had become the subject of a monumental scandal which led to Margaret's downfall.

When I switched on the tape recorder on 16 April 1974 she began to recall the unbelievable story of her life, revealing details she had previously kept secret. Her first words were careful and hesitant because of her stammer. She said much, perhaps unwisely, as she had been restrained from uttering certain slanders by a court order and could have landed in prison were she to repeat them.

Margaret always wanted to dance with me. Her first husband Charles Sweeny danced like Astaire. She knew that I had been a professional stage and television dancer after the style of Gene Kelly and that I liked dancing. Despite my caution, three months later, she proved how deceitful she really was and I became another victim of the lies for which she was so well known. It was often difficult to discern when she was lying or telling the truth. I believe that she, herself, was sometimes confused about what was fact and what fantasy.

It all proved fascinating listening although much of what she told me could not be published for libel reasons. Margaret's vitriolic remarks about people in high office whom she knew illustrated the sort of woman she was.

For all that, her story was compelling, and she told it in words evocative of the thirties, the period of her fame.

Her speech patterns and phraseology brought her past to life – even if her account was unreliable. She had, after all, been branded a poisonous liar in court.

Margaret always wanted to be a star, and she became one – a star of courtrooms and tabloids. Her role was always that of the heroine and she made everyone else seem the villain.

Margaret might have been a woman of straw, but you couldn't help liking her: she was elegant, poised, well dressed and had impeccable manners in society. She enjoyed being addressed as 'Your Grace' by lesser folk, had no respect for people and less for the law. She could be rude, off-handed and insulting to those who served her. The stories told against her by beauticians, *vendeuses*, restaurant waiters and hotel staff are legion. When once asked by a journalist: 'Do you enjoy being a Duchess?', she replied without hesitation: 'Who doesn't?'

—CHARLES CASTLE

CHAPTER ONE

The Bad Seed

'GOD knows he was an old bastard,' said the Duchess. She was referring to the High Court judge who had awarded her husband a divorce on the grounds of her adultery, and who had concluded that 'The Duchess is wholly immoral.' He also recorded that she was promiscuous. She had been branded a liar by Queen's Counsel at a previous trial and her husband had referred to her as 'S' – Satan.

The Duke named three men as co-respondents in his action against her and Margaret counter-petitioned against him in vain. Stories had circulated in London that she kept pornographic diaries in which she awarded her lovers star ratings based on their sexual abilities. It was proved that she had indecent photographs of herself with other men, taken during her marriage to the Duke, which he seized from her at night while she was asleep. In summing up, the judge, Lord Wheatley, took four and a half hours to deliver 64,000 words. 'The photographs not only establish that the Duchess was carrying on an adulterous association with an unknown man or men but they also reveal that the Duchess is a highly sexed woman who had ceased to be satisfied with normal relations and had started to indulge in what I can only describe as disgusting sexual activities to gratify her sexual appetite.'

The woman who became the Duchess of Argyll had loved the man she married in 1951 but love turned to hate on both sides after four embittered years. She believed that the husband who had once cherished her finally tricked, attacked and humiliated her. But he did so for several good reasons. She believed that there was a dirty-tricks campaign to drive her out of society after she had married the Duke. She was also aware that it was a dirty, treacherous and lengthy tangle with the truth. Yet it was she alone who was the instigator of the poison-pen letters, slanders and intrigue wrought on the name of the Argyll family that led to the many legal actions that ensued. Margaret entered into the foray with relish. She knew it would lead to endless time taken up with lawyers and counsel, with private detectives whom she employed to trail some of her enemies and others who shadowed her and bugged her hired car in New York, incurring costs that would have crippled Fort Knox. Something in her nature drove her on without fear to do precisely what she wanted no matter the price or the consequence.

Margaret Whigham was born in Scotland on 1 December 1912. She was described in the press as the greatest débutante of all time before she reached the age of eighteen and by the thirties was a celebrated beauty. The tide turned on the fashionable and successful party-goer when her first marriage to the handsome John Kennedy look-alike and much sought-after London-based Irish-American Charles Sweeny ended in divorce.

As the only child of millionaire parents who provided her with comfort, shielded her from the realities of life and lavished limitless money on her she grew up to possess not only enviable beauty and grace, but every conceivable material advantage.

Yet Margaret's girlhood was an empty shell. She had no friends with whom to play and laugh, share jokes or to invent stories. There was no sharing of any kind, of either toys or emotions. Like a parrot in a gilded cage, she chirped away but attracted no loving response except admiration and pride of possession. She was fed and provided for, but she was never taught to love, and never learnt the importance and satisfaction of true and honest emotion. She was never taught respect for anyone outside her family.

'My father George Hay Whigham was one of ten children,' Margaret, Duchess of Argyll began. 'His father, David Dundas Whigham, was a Scots county squire of considerable charm, but the possessor of very little money. He was, however, a proud man determined that his sons would do well, which indeed they did.

'Father's eldest brother Robert became General on Foch's staff in the first war and was subsequently knighted. Four of my uncles became millionaires including my father. Jim, the second eldest, although he never made a great deal of money, had an interesting life as a roving reporter and finally became editor of the American magazine *Town and Country*. The other three were Charles, a partner of Morgan Grenfell, one of the great financing houses in England and America, who helped to negotiate the Anglo-American loan after the First World War; Gilbert, head of the Burmah Oil Company; and Walter, Director of the Bank of England, the richest of them all. My father George founded and became chairman of the multi-million-pound Celanese man-made fibre empire after helping to build the Canadian Pacific and Cuban Railways under Sir William van Horen.'

Margaret's family were all true-blue God-fearing Presbyterians. On her father's side the line goes back to the twelfth century when Helias de Dundas was granted the lands of Dundas in Scotland by King David I. The Dundas men remained prominent down the centuries, one as judge of the Court of Session in 1662, then his son Sir Robert Dundas, who rose to the bench, and his grandson who became Solicitor-General for Scotland. (Perhaps it is no wonder that Margaret became so enmeshed in the law since it had been in the family's blood for so long.) The next generation produced another Robert, who became Lord Advocate and then Lord President. Born on 22 August 1832, Margaret's grandfather, David Dundas Whigham, came of the ancient Scottish legal line from Dumfriesshire near Glasgow. He was the immediate founder of Margaret's family and son of Robert Whigham of Lochpatrick, an advocate and Sheriff of Perthshire, who married the only daughter of Sir Robert Dundas in 1824, Jane. He was an exacting man with cast-iron determination and his sons knew they would have much to answer for if they should fail to make a success of their lives.

Margaret's paternal grandmother, Ellen, was the daughter of James Campbell and Grace Hay. Ellen and David Dundas Whigham married in 1864 and a year later gave birth to their first child, Robert, who became a well-liked soldier. Nine other children were born in rapid succession – four girls and six boys, the last of whom, George Hay, Margaret's father, was born on 24 September 1879. After the costly education of the first-born boys and supporting a family of twelve, the family's money ran out and Margaret's father began his career by serving a five-year apprenticeship in the civil engineering firm of Formans & McCall in Glasgow at a starting salary of thirty shillings a week. After the turn of the century, he found work in designing and costing at Renfrew Dock followed by the Highland Water Power Scheme and the High Level Bascule Bridge over Glasgow Harbour and later became involved in the design of material for the steel pier at Almeria in Spain. His worthy treatise *Whigham on Light Railways*, published in 1902, was read before the Institute of Civil Engineers in Glasgow and resulted in his being appointed resident engineer on the Lanarkshire and Ayrshire Railway where, with a budget of £750,000, he became responsible for the design and execution of bridges, tunnels and stations. There would appear to have been no room for love in the life of a man so dedicated to his profession but he lost his heart to a pretty young Scots lass, who became Margaret's mother.

A copper magnate and his wife lived in a large house called Broome at Newton Mearns in Renfrewshire. Their daughter Helen Marion was jealously guarded by her parents, who were highly suspicious of any suitor. By 1905 George Hay Whigham was twenty-six years old and had thoughts of marriage, but, although industrious and with good prospects, he was practically penniless and thus not acceptable to the wealthy Hannays as a suitable match for Helen, despite his charm and ardour. However, George had been offered an appointment in Egypt with the Wardan

Estate Company and was about to leave Scotland to take up a five-year contract. He wanted desperately to do so with a new young wife by his side.

'That was a very romantic story, my mother's runaway marriage with him,' Margaret said. 'This very rich girl and this poor boy. She was rich because her father, my grandfather, was a copper millionaire by the name of Douglas Hannay. My own father was extremely difficult, obviously very bright from an amazing family of ten. He was going around all the parties outside Glasgow on the Clyde where all the people congregated, the industrial set who were going strong. The Williamses, the Sainsburys, the Inverclydes and the Weirs, they were all Scots from that part of the world. Very rich, very successful and they gave lots of parties. My father met and fell in love with my mother straight away at one of those parties. She was an awfully pretty woman; and also very petite, like a sort of doll. They adored one another. But he hadn't any money. He lived on an allowance from my grandfather in Glasgow of thirty bob a week, about ten pounds at the time. Very little. He was a civil engineer, learning to be a chartered accountant at night school. Obviously very intelligent. Then he came to ask my grandfather whether he could marry my mother. She was a very spoilt girl. Had her own maid, got her coats from Paris. And my grandfather said, "All right, you're going to Egypt. If you come back earning five hundred pounds a year you can marry my daughter" – thinking, he could never do that, and bye-bye, George Whigham, I'll never hear from you again. And off he went to Egypt. Months later my grandfather saw a letter from my father on the table at breakfast. He knew what it was, that my father was coming back to ask for her because by now he was making five hundred a year and was returning on leave after six months in Egypt. But my grandfather said, "All right, she can marry him but she's not going to get a penny from me." He didn't trust my father. He thought he was marrying her for her money. So my mother said, "Fine. I couldn't care less. I love him and I'm going."'

The runaway heiress and the young adventurer married and soon after 'they went to live in the desert. She had two dresses a year and a hat, and she couldn't care less. She adored him.' Margaret inherited her mother's headstrong, defiant nature but not her sense of economy. It was usual for Margaret to acquire five day dresses, five cocktail dresses and five ballgowns every season. She also inherited her father's charm, adventurous spirit and his philosophy of never taking no for an answer.

Margaret inherited her mother's beauty and vanity, too, and her ability to get what she wanted. She knew that her mother had found happiness by deserting her parents and running off with the penniless man she loved. This callous streak in her mother, the ability to cause family friction

8

so early in her life, was another trait that showed itself in Margaret when she fell out in later life with her own daughter, Frances, and her grandchildren.

Whilst Margaret learnt her lack of respect for authority from her mother, she grasped the nature of greed and avarice from her father although he never succeeded in teaching her the value of money. She learnt only how to spend it – which is an art in itself. She also derived her social ambition from him. Margaret was his most prized possession and although all were allowed to admire, he did not want to part with it at any price. Father and daughter were deeply devoted to one another, but Margaret had no room in her life for her mother whom she felt stood between them. She could not understand that the love she demanded from her father rightly belonged to her mother. Just as she never shared her toys, she never shared her father.

The newly-weds spent the first four years of their married life in Egypt in which time George fulfilled his contract. By the time he was thirty he had managed to save over £10,000 through both his industry as a civil engineer and his accounting skills. During this period his brother Walter was employed by the finance company Robert Fleming and Co. in New York. In 1911 he encouraged George and Helen to join him in America and secured for George a job in the employ of Sir William van Horen in the construction of the Cuban Railroad. After his death the ambitious young George succeeded van Horen as president.

One of George's other brothers, James, a former war correspondent with three worthy books on the Far East and golf to his credit, had joined the staff of the *London Standard* as foreign editor. He remained there for two years until 1908 when he became editor of both the *Metropolitan* magazine and *Town and Country* in New York. He provided George and Helen with accommodation in his smart apartment, and their home became the United States. Feeling settled for the first time since running away with George, Helen found herself pregnant. She became homesick, having spent almost five years away from her family and roots, and yearned to give birth near her mother, besides wanting the child to be born on Scottish soil. She also felt confident of forgiveness now that George had more than proved his essential worth. They returned to Scotland to the Hannay home, Broome, in Renfrewshire.

Her parents, however, were still angry with their wayward daughter, their disapproval justified when they realized that Helen had not come home for their sake but for her own. They were further incensed when they learnt that Helen would be returning to America once the child was born. They knew that they were being used. It ran in the blood.

On 1 December 1912 the Whighams' only child, Ethel Margaret, burst on an unsuspecting world.

CHAPTER TWO

Dance, Little Lady

W HEN Margaret was a month old her parents returned to New York and there they stayed.

'Of course I was too young to remember the Great War years but I do remember the celebration of Armistice they had in America. Everyone was yelling and cheering but I didn't know what they were yelling about. I recall, too, an old HMV record playing, "Over There", "The Yanks are Coming" and "It's a Long, Long Winding Trail".

'My earliest memories of being a child were the sounds of the sirens of ships going up and down the river, no doubt because we lived in a duplex apartment near Central Park and the sounds were very loud and clear.'

Margaret acquired an American accent but little education.

However, attempts to alter her speech to upper-class English with her mother's eye to the future of her pride and joy were to prove abundantly fruitful in time.

Brearley, the school to which Margaret was first sent in New York, proved too advanced for her and on a visit to Britain in 1920 when she was eight her mother decided that an English nanny would be the most suitable way in which to rear her child. The family was staying at the Ritz Hotel in London, *en route* to visit the Hannays in Scotland, and it was here that Helen interviewed several prospective English nannies. The successful applicant was Nurse May Randall, who became the devoted servant until she married many years later. When they concluded their holiday in Scotland the three Whighams with Nanny May sailed back to New York.

As Margaret was brought up by her nanny she never became close to her mother. As an only child, surrounded by toys and cuddly teddy bears, she learnt to rely on the inanimate objects for comfort. Her mother and father were Victorian and strict Presbyterian Scots. Any strong display of emotion would have been alien to them and Margaret's memories were always of material comforts rather than of parents who provided love and affirmation. Her mother showed her none of the caring for which she craved. Later in life Margaret would be guilty of the same cold, callous lack of emotion in her own dealings with people – both friends and family.

'I was sent to a very famous school in New York after my first attempt at education there, which my father had helped to found. It was begun by an English woman by the name of Miss Hewitt who was a governess. She had managed to get four or five of the children's fathers to finance it. George F. Baker was one and my father was another. But I nearly got expelled because I won three prizes in a row (through cheating). Greek history, Egyptian history and world history. In order to win them I had to write and find a picture for an album and in order to get a certain good one I got a library book, cut the picture out, put the book back on its shelf and stuck it in my album. When they discovered what I had done I was sent away under a very black cloud and I just shrugged the whole thing off and said, "*Ça va.*" Then when I went back in the autumn I found that everyone else had cut pictures out of the library books as well!'

Two of her closest friends at this establishment were Gloria, daughter of the famous Italian tenor, Enrico Caruso, and the Woolworths heiress Barbara Hutton, with whom in later life Margaret shared an insatiable enjoyment of men and money.

The reason for Barbara Hutton's lifelong search for love and longevity might easily have been attributed to the fact that her mother had flung herself from a window committing suicide but Margaret's reason for her own choice of lifestyle in later years was conceivably more complex.

She was unacquainted with the irregular verb 'to love'.

When women love deeply they give of themselves whole-heartedly. They would sacrifice their lives and forsake their own children and friends for the man they cherish. By and large, Margaret's love was unrequited. She never found such a man for whom she would give her soul. She loved her father deeply, but that was a different kind of love.

She came to realize that the love men feel was more akin to her own emotions. Theirs is, by and large, a physical, practical love, lacking in huge sacrifice. Men hold on to what they have created and built up for reasons of self-protection. To give is to gamble, and, therefore, possibly lose. Margaret shared this same sort of male caution.

Later she would love the man by whom she had two children, Charles Sweeny. But the love she felt for him was similar to his own practical, no-nonsense kind of love. When he went off the rails, so did she. It was quid pro quo.

She would never trust a man again after he had betrayed her love. Like his, her love was physical.

Her need for security stemmed from the fact that she had always had it and feared losing it. She had never worked for a living for one day in her life.

In consequence, she never really understood or appreciated the true value of anything in life. Neither spiritually, emotionally nor financially.

*

During this time Margaret's father was heavily involved in the construction of the Canadian Pacific Railway while gaining ground in the area which made him his fortune, the development of Celanese fibre, with the support of his brother Walter. The young family continued to spend their annual holidays travelling to Europe where George Whigham had met the inventors of the new fabric in Zurich.

In sharp contrast to her father's activities, Margaret's mother was concerned about her fourteen-year-old daughter's future. 'The reason my mother came back here to Britain was because at that time all the kids who had become kind of débutantes in New York had been getting terribly drunk, and they were lying around on the sofas out like lights on the very bad stuff they were giving them. Although my mother had visions of me getting drunk, actually I never drank anything. So they brought me to England where they took a house at Ascot.'

The manor house that the Whighams took in this highly fashionable area of Berkshire was called Queen's Hill; it was set in thirty acres of land facing the world-famous racecourse and they gave house-parties during the racing season. When they were in London they lived in a rented house in South Audley Street in Mayfair.

'We had been coming backwards and forwards after the war every summer by then and I had crossed the Atlantic fourteen times by the time I was eleven years old. To me it was like taking a train to Glasgow. Although it became terribly boring it was very exciting to other children to get on the *Carmania*, the *Olympic* or the *Mauretania* – but to me it was absolute peanuts.

'One of my greatest difficulties in leaving America was because of my teddy bears. I couldn't have any live animals in New York so I had my teddy bears which I loved. Brownie, Blackie and Teddy. They were so much loved and kissed that I had kissed them bare. I used to make little coats for them. They had their own wardrobe trunk, hangers, chest of drawers, bed, pram, cot. Their own luggage. And once my father said, "I'm damned if I'll travel with those blessed bears' luggage any more." And I said, "In that case, I don't go." We had a confrontation over me and my teddies at a very early age and I won.'

When they returned to England permanently, Margaret's education was of prime importance but remained patchy. She was sent first to one of London's most fashionable private schools in South Audley Street under the tutelage of Miss Woolf, who taught the Duke of Norfolk's sisters, Lord Curzon's daughter (who became Baroness Ravensdale) and Jeanne Stourton who later married Lord Camoys's only son, the Hon. Sherman Stonor. Two others were Cecil Beaton's sisters, Baba and Nancy. She went for dancing lessons to Madame Vacani whose privilege it was to teach the waltz and quick-step to Princess Elizabeth and Princess Margaret Rose, and later to Prince Charles, Princess Anne, lesser royalty and the aristocracy.

Margaret was then dispatched to the exclusive girls' school Heathfield as a day-girl, 'And I hated it. It must have shown because I wasn't very popular. I couldn't abide boarding schools for girls. I was a spoilt only child, more sophisticated than the others, and when I was collected in a chauffeur-driven car to be taken back home to Queen's Hill in Ascot every day, I'd say, "Bye-bye, you poor things, playing in your galoshes and white tunics." I had no *esprit de corps*, and certainly didn't want to play hockey or lacrosse or cricket with anybody.' Her sporting activities were confined to the indoor variety for many years to come.

'I don't like women in a mass. I think they should be individuals. And these girls were being told constantly when to wash their hair. And I kept telling them to *stop* being told when to do so. I was then asked to either conform or to leave. So I left. I went after only a year. My parents were always trying to get me out of England to Europe, to Austria or Switzerland to have a healthy, outdoor life because I was growing up too fast.

'Then I was sent to a fashionable finishing school in Paris run exclusively for English girls which I equally loathed. It was called Ausanne. Run by Madame Ausanne.

I was there for three ghastly months. And that was the end of that!

'Education was never my strong point. I absorbed a great deal from being with grown-ups, though. That's how I learnt. I heard them talking and I used to listen quite hard. I never liked people of my own age, ever. I preferred older people and I simply adored being an only child. Adored it. The greatest threat you could give me was when my mother used to say, "If you're naughty, you'll have a little brother or sister." And I used to say, "Anything, anything but that!" I was completely self-sufficient.

'In her way my mother was very selfish. She was a strange mixture. She was extremely unselfish to my father and married him on nothing. She adored him. He was the love of her life and she helped him build up his vast empire. She could get people to communicate with her. If you were talking to her you'd be telling her your all.

'I don't think I look particularly like her. I don't look like either parent. Perhaps my grandmother. My mother's mother was a very beautiful woman. She had the green eyes which I have. My parents both had blue eyes. My mother was tiny. She was very petite. About five feet two. And everything to match. She had tiny hands, tiny feet. Like a doll. And she was terribly funny about herself. She had a tremendous sense of humour but in her way she was very selfish. But she was also loyal and she was extremely spoilt in her way. She had tremendous charm. She could charm a bird off a tree and she was absolutely un-shy. That's where I get it from. I have never been shy.

'She was a very open person. Very uncomplicated and easily impressed by anyone or anything. And she was very fey. They call the Scots fey. She'd had absolutely no education. Talk about *me* having none, she had less. But she was very spoiled and accustomed to being the centre of attention. She was one of three children. She had a brother, and a sister who was very pretty and chic. Beautifully dressed and groomed, she was a very active person who played golf and tennis. My mother was supposed to be the ugly duckling but she wasn't ugly at all. She could also be very moody. If she'd had a bad night, you couldn't make a noise the next morning. She was extremely good at running the house and the servants adored her. But she was tough with them, much tougher than I've ever been. She was very spoiled and accustomed to being the centre of attention but although she was almost illiterate she had the most extraordinary instinct. You couldn't lie to her or fool her. She had an X-ray mind, which my father hadn't. My father who was a very charming and brilliant man was very tough in business but he was awfully gullible. Which I am. Very gullible. They fool you every time. He'd ask my mother about something, about a partner or a director of the firm and say to her, "He's very nice. He's very respectable. He's got credentials." And my mother would say, "Don't touch him. I don't like him. He's a crook." She had extraordinary perceptiveness which I haven't got. As I said, I do have my father's gull—gull—[another hesitation, then] gullibility.'

Margaret inherited her occasional stammer from neither parent and hard though she tried to conquer it throughout her life she never succeeded. Yet, strangely enough, as she grew older this inability to speak fluidly lent its own attraction. Men felt she lacked confidence and offered her a supportive arm on which to lean. It became one of her compelling yet unwitting charms, a dangerous spell for those who fell for her *façade* of vulnerability.

Her mother had explained that unless she managed to overcome her impediment she would achieve little in life, and although this advice was meant constructively the psychological effect of it worsened the problem. Despite visits to specialists in New York and London, and a final effort by speech therapist Lionel Logue who treated King George VI, she retained this imperfection in an otherwise glittering life. No one realized that the cause stemmed from Margaret's having been born left-handed and always forced to use the right which led to marked physical and psychological feelings of inadequacy. Her mother's final advice, when it was discovered that Logue could do nothing for Margaret, was to persevere. Helen warned that a hard road lay ahead of a girl so worldly, charming, beautiful and, probably, richer than other girls of similar background unless she redress this imbalance. Margaret could become a recluse unless she learnt to fight her handicap: if she ran away from life because of this blight she would meet fewer and fewer people, be unable to answer the telephone and find herself incapable of conducting herself confidently, ending up lonely and desperate for company.

Yet the stammer was not only caused by feelings of inadequacy: there is no doubt that being the only child of a cold distant mother and a doting but absent father played their part in undermining Margaret's sense of security. That she did eventually become lonely, desperate and outcast from society at the height of her beauty and social acclaim was for reasons unconnected with the speech impediment.

'My mother did the awful thing of telling me about sex. I wish to God she had shut up. You don't know about it but you don't want to hear about it. And her attitude was, "It's this awful thing we women have to put up with. We close our eyes and bear it." And I just didn't want to know. I was extremely independent as a child, perfectly happy to be left alone, which was rather rare, but I was always very busy.

'My father and I were very much alike. We were both arguers. He taught me how to argue, which you do without anger, or anybody banging doors or raising voices. He taught me to argue pros and cons and my mother couldn't understand this at all… People loved him. He was a very good employer. He would have been a very good Labour leader although he wasn't particularly politically minded. He was all for Roosevelt in the days when everybody thought that Roosevelt was very far left. My father was always for the worker.

'My parents had a very good time together, really. They were obviously fond of one another. He was a very good-looking man but he was very unfaithful to her and made her unhappy at times. She went off and left him once with me. We were in Biarritz for the winter, as I remember it, and she'd had enough. But my father pleaded and got her back.'

George had spent the previous six years in America developing the revolutionary new man-made fibre Celanese. The industry expanded rapidly into Canada and Britain and, through his hard work, he became chairman of the company in all three countries. This was not achieved through tenacity alone but also through his extraction of the patent from the control of the Swiss inventors.

'There were three scientists who came from Zurich. They were called Dreyfus. There was Dr Oriol Dreyfus, Dr Camille Dreyfus and then there was Dr Henry Dreyfus. They invented a thing which was called viscose-acetate which was a man-made substance that came out of a tube. And that was artificial silk. It was the first time that it was ever invented. It was before Dupont. This was the first and they called it Celanese. My father discovered the Dreyfuses. He was a very far-seeing man and he foresaw the future of this which was rather extraordinary. It was in 1921 or so. He told them he would put it on the market because they didn't have a clue how to go about doing so. So he said, 'Just keep on inventing', and he would see to the rest. And so that's how Celanese was born. The rivals, Courtaulds, called theirs Melanese and they were the two big beginners of artificial silk. Up to then people were in lisle and raw silk stockings. Nobody ever knew about anything else. So my father put every egg he had in that basket which was quite a gamble.

'And I remember him bringing home some ugly, shiny stuff. Hideous. Horribly shiny, and he said, "These are going to be our curtains," and my mother said, "Over my dead body." Then I remember in 1926 seeing the front page of the *Evening Standard*, not the back pages where the business items were, but on the front page. The shares went from six shillings to six pounds overnight. It leapt. And my father had made it.

'Courtaulds were very close behind with Melanese, and a long time afterwards came Dupont which meant Orlon, Nylon and Terylene. And, of course, what they made their fortunes on were things like parachutes, rafts, lifeboats and canvas for sailing ships. It wasn't our stockings and drapes on which they made their fortune.

'And then came the Wall Street crash in 1929 but my father didn't lose much in the crash because he saw what was coming. He was in New York and he went around one Sunday in August and saw every other flat was to let or to sell. And he knew at once there was going to be a crash and he got out. This was the sort of foresight he had and he managed to escape without losing much.'

In 1930 Margaret 'came out'. Although the official coming-out age was eighteen, since Margaret was born in December she came out when she was seventeen and a half. Her coming-out dance took place at 6 Audley Square, where the Whighams had rented a house for the season, a fortnight before she was to be presented at Court. But the joyous occasion was threatened with disaster. Granny Hannay had come from Scotland to join in the festivities but fell dangerously ill forty-eight hours before the guests were expected to converge on the house. Near panic resulted, with Margaret collapsing into the depths of despair. Her nerves fraught, she dropped the cake baked specially for the staff when she carried it to the kitchen. Old, frail, thin and weak, there seemed little chance for old Mrs Hannay and on the morning of the ball her breathing grew weaker. However, with true Scots courage and the cast-iron determination that had flowed in the family's blood since time immemorial, she rallied, and when Ambrose's band struck up as a galaxy of guests spilled through the entrance,

Margaret appeared, radiant in a pale blue crinoline dress with a tight-fitting bodice shimmering with diamanté, translucent crystals and pearls.

Margaret was thankful for her grandmother's timely recovery not because the grandmother she hardly knew survived her setback, but because her well-organized party could go ahead.

'My coming-out dance was one of the most wonderful evenings of my life. We had invited over four hundred people and I remember the thrill of reading all about it in the papers the next day. "Miss Whigham, one of the loveliest débutantes of the year," reported one newspaper, "shone out above everybody else, as is only fitting for the heroine of such an evening, radiant in a blue-green crinoline dress." And another, "Miss Whigham stood out from a row of débutantes like a thoroughbred in a field of hacks."'

She was undeniably beautiful, but Margaret stood out in a different way from the hordes of other débutantes wearing their obligatory white dresses. Margaret, too, had been told by her parents that she would wear white, but, ever wilful, she intentionally stained her skirt just hours before the event and therefore emerged triumphant in the peacock blue ensemble which set her apart from her rivals.

'We spent the time between the house in Ascot, which we had until I married, and London. We had great fun giving Ascot house-parties. But I preferred London with its gaiety, but for all that, we were terribly heavily chaperoned. When you were at a party, every girl was asked with her mother. But, of course, a lot of mothers cried off. My mother would say, "For God's sake, do we have to go to another one of those?" It was one, two or three a night. And you always asked the girl and her mother.

'Of course it was tricky getting *men*. None of us were meant to have men. Mothers were meant to give dinners, and bowl them all along. The mothers would sit on a gold chair, which my mother wasn't too keen on doing, so she'd say, "Now, look, if I send the car and chauffeur back do you promise to come home by ten? Because I'm off!" I wasn't allowed out with a man alone for the first year that I came out. There always had to be four or six of us. And my nanny, who really brought me up and whom I loved much more than my mother, used to always be sent out with me all day and often had to wait in the car all evening. I was never allowed out on my own in the daytime either. Isn't it extraordinary to think of it? Nobody worked either. No girl worked. She went to school, came out and got married. The young men had time to spare; the young Guards officers, for instance. It was another world.

'And then I got engaged at seventeen to Prince Aly Khan. It was great love at first sight, and I was engaged to him the first summer I came out. I first saw him when I was presented at Court. My mother and I arrived at the

Palace and were shown into the ante-room. When my mother's name was announced, I followed her into the Throne Room where the diplomats were resplendent in their Court dress and the women magnificent in their jewels. Thankfully, a terrifying hush was broken by the music from the string orchestra in the gallery, and I was presented to Queen Mary, who naturally dominated the scene. I made my curtsy, and as I looked up, I saw this strikingly handsome boy standing directly behind the Queen, wearing a pure white Indian outfit buttoned to the neck. He had large black eyes, and a white turban with a huge green emerald in front of it. I looked at him and he looked at me, and then I passed on down the line. It was the next night that I met him at a party given for the Mountbattens. Sir Ernest Cassells gave the party in his house for Edwina Mountbatten. I remember Aly and I danced all night at this party, and all night at every other party.

'I went to my first Derby with him, when his father's horse, Blenheim, won the big race; and Aly stayed with us at Queen's Hill for my first Ascot.

'And then he came and asked my father for my hand, and my father nearly had a fit.

'I was far too young, only seventeen and a half, and he was Persian. Of course, Aly didn't forgive him for this. "I want to marry you," he said. "I couldn't do more than ask for that. I don't know why your father wouldn't agree." Of course, I would have married him had my father agreed. Then we were forbidden to meet. But we used to meet in the gardens of dances and parties. Secretly. We used to go to the Embassy Club, where I was made an honorary member a few years later, which was *the* club to go to, and everybody went wearing white-tie. Afterwards he'd go there alone and ask the band to play the tunes he remembered that we used to dance to. It was all very romantic. He was terribly attractive at that time. He was slim and had this black hair. An awfully sweet person and he had the most charming manners.'

He also had guile. He would arrange for them to dine with mutual friends and while Margaret's guardian chauffeur waited at the front door, they would slip off via the servants' entrance to the Embassy Club, where they danced the night away.

Young love for her suitor was condemned by her father but she was too attached to George to marry against his wishes. She could easily have followed in her wilful mother's footsteps and married anyway, but her love and respect for her father ran deeper. Prince Aly Khan finally married one of Lord Churston's daughters, Joan. (Her other three sisters became Duchess of Bedford, the Countess of Cadogan and Lady Ebury.) Years later he eloped with and married Rita Hayworth.

One of the reasons the Whighams chose Ascot to live was because George's main pastime was golf and the proximity of the course to Queen's Hill was ideal. Queen's Hill was also near London.

'They tried to keep me *out* of London, but all I did was spend my time on the road, to and fro. And it was also near all my friends at Eton, Oxford and an awful lot of other people in the houses round that area. Ascot at that time was very chic. Very "in". The Ascot house-parties were great fun. You had the Guards Ball; I can't remember all you *did* have, but there were always two or three private dances being given, and the Guards Ball was tremendous to be asked to. And people didn't go down for the day as they do nowadays, they went for the week travelling with their own valet or private maid. And you had three different dresses for each day. The whole thing was quite extraordinary. I had a tremendous lot of clothes. I helped to make Norman Hartnell and Victor Stiebel. They were beginners from Cambridge and then both got to Bruton Street in London. And I was in *everything, everywhere*. My mother and I didn't go to Paris for our clothes. We bought everything in London. We had everything here, so why go there? We had Molyneux, Worth, the lot. Hartnell made my presentation dress, my wedding dress, everything. He made beautiful clothes.

'The period between 1930 and 1933 was packed with gaiety and fun and nobody can take that away from me. It was heaven. Undiluted heaven. Fun. Three parties a night. Not a serious thought in my head. Featherbrained. Blissful. I don't think anybody has had such a good time as I had. Nobody, nobody, nobody. And my parents did everything to make it fun for me. I had clothes, I had money behind me, which my father was an angel about. I could ask for practically everything I wanted. Two big parties given in three years for me with over four hundred guests on each occasion which must have cost at least £40,000 for each party (it would cost £150,000 nowadays). One was given up here in London, and the other down at Ascot. It was a constant ball. And thank God I've had it.'

The incomparable Sir Noël Coward composed one of his most enduring songs, 'Dance Little Lady', describing that frenzied period. The lyrics relate to Margaret's carefree philosophy and love of life so well that he might easily have composed them with her in mind with its warning against too much wildness.

Margaret was in the public eye from this early age and would remain the pinnacle of interest to her own delight as much as to that of her many admirers. Rich, young, beautiful, always elegantly dressed, and expensively yet discreetly bejewelled, she had exquisite manners and taste. She became the débutante of the season, much photographed and favourably reported in the press, and was said to be the first to hire a press agent – though this was hotly denied – financed by her ambitious father. (Any amount of publicity he could attract for his treasured child would reflect on the price of Celanese shares.) Rumours circulated that Charles Lyttle (pronounced Lightly), the public relations man, was seen in deep conversation on many occasions with George Whigham at the Dorchester Hotel, a stone's throw from George's Mayfair residence.

'My father was accused of hiring a press agent for me, and there could be nothing further from the truth. He couldn't understand it, but he didn't mind it. There was nothing harmful in it. Oddly enough, my father and mother weren't at all ambitious. If they had been, they'd have urged me to marry Prince Aly Khan and encouraged me to marry Fulke Warwick which would have made me the Countess of Warwick.'

Her parents' 'lack of ambition' for her was not as simple as Margaret believed. They were, in fact, desperately ambitious. In the case of Prince Aly Khan, their reasons for refusing him were racist. In Warwick's case, they played no part: the couple mutually agreed to call it a day when they realized that Fulke had fallen in love with another woman and Margaret had become smitten with the dashing Charles Sweeny.

The *ingénue* resented being referred to as the 'Débutante of the Year' because she considered herself to rank in far higher echelons. 'I was actually supposed to be a second

Lady Diana Cooper,' she had the effrontery to say, comparing herself to one of the most unique women in society, the most beautiful of several generations. 'She was a great star in her era.' The late Duke of Rutland's daughter, Lady Diana Cooper, whose remarkable beauty was renowned for over fifty years, was described by *Vogue* as 'untarnishable, the loveliest young Englishwoman of her generation'. 'To enumerate Lady Diana's virtues is to risk being accused of exaggeration or prejudice,' said Sir Cecil Beaton. 'Yet who does not warrant high praise if not a beauty who is a wit, an enlightening *raconteuse*, and a brilliant correspondent (it may well be that she will live in posterity by her letters)? She is an artist in life with countless artistic gifts, a friend with unswerving loyalties, at once business-like, capable, imaginative and full of heartbreak, an eccentric who is frank and outspoken with the knowledge of when not to mention any given subject.' Lady Diana seemed to have been a woman with most of the rare qualities that Margaret so desperately wanted to acquire. In the event Margaret became related to her, albeit distantly, when her daughter Frances married Charles, the 10th Duke of Rutland, Lady Diana's nephew.

'The thing about débutantes at that time,' Margaret continued, 'was that they were in it with an eye to the future, which was pretty ghastly, and all the young men used to run from them like rabbits till I came myself and was so terribly international. I wore make-up, nail-polish, and was extremely well dressed. I used to buy six to seven evening dresses at a go from the top London couturiers. I was out every night, and nobody dressed like I did. There were three of us. Bridget Crawlett and Rose Bennet. We all burst on the world at the same time in 1930. We hit London such as it had never been hit before. Bridget and I were great friends but although Rose was terribly attractive, I never liked her much. She was the sort of girl who, in those days, was tremendously risky. She announced that she was going to have twenty-one affairs by the time she was twenty-one. And did. And she made no bones about it because she was extremely, well, *sassy*. Although she was very well bred she looked what she was. Good-looking and available. She was great fun and very amusing, but she was never a friend of mine. She finally married the Earl of Warwick to whom I was engaged for a short while.

'There was a middle-page spread in the *Sunday Express*, a leading article written by the editor who said that you can't find faces other than these three. And we went on for three years until we were married. Nothing was complete without us. And then the press started to say, "We'll invent something of our own. We're not going to have these three constantly in front of us." And so they championed another débutante by the name of Primrose and planted a photograph of her in the paper practically every day and she faded after the first season because she hadn't got what we had. It was very nebulous. Very intangible. I suppose it was star quality. And I have to talk about myself objectively, because that was what I had.

'A lot of people will hate me to death for saying so, but I had a knack of projecting myself, producing myself. Almost like an actress. I was the one that lasted. The others faded after three years. There was another one, Rosemary Cook, but she and Bridget Crawlett faded too.

'I was my own little star in a very social world.'

The little star shone so brightly as to dazzle some of the most eligible bachelors in town including not only Aly Khan and Fulke Warwick but Max Aitken, the newspaper tycoon Lord Beaverbrook's son. At the same time, she also enjoyed romances with two other men, the first of whom was already married, which set a pattern for the many married men to whom she was attracted once she became Duchess of Argyll.

'The millionaire sportsman and pioneer aviator Commander Glen Kidson used to take me out. This was in 1931, the year after I came out. He was tall, very attractive and about thirty-five. On the eve of his departure on a solo flight to the Cape, I went out with him and Richard Norton, the present Lord Grantley's father, and another girl. He dropped me back at the Ritz, where I was staying, and gave me absolutely no indication of how he really felt. Imagine my surprise, when the following morning, after he had gone, I received a letter from him and a beautiful diamond wrist-watch. The letter said that he had been in love with me for many months and asked me to marry him when he was free. He was not yet divorced.

'He cabled me on his arrival in Cape Town saying, "I have done it, Margaret." I knew then that he had broken the record. But one evening later I read in the evening newspaper headlines that Glen had been killed making an impromptu sightseeing flight over Table Mountain.

'Imagine the shock and sadness I felt when his letters kept arriving by sea-mail for at least a month after his death outlining plans for our marriage and future together.'

Her sadness was compounded by guilt because she had already started going out with the handsome young American, Charles Sweeny, but she became engaged to Max Aitken shortly after. Ironically – as it later transpired – his sister Janet Aitken was married to Captain Ian Campbell who, on the death of his cousin, became Duke of Argyll and Margaret's second husband. 'I didn't know Ian at the time but when he was dining with his first wife Janet at the Café de Paris, he saw me coming down those famous stairs and said to her, "That's the girl I'm going to marry some day." Needless to say *that* marriage didn't last much longer after a remark like that.

'And then the following year in 1932 when I was nineteen my mother and father wanted to go to Egypt for the winter, which was the fashionable thing for the British to do in those days. It wasn't until years later that it became *comme il faut* to spend the winter in the South of France. Of course, I was having such a lovely time in London that I didn't want to go but I was simply told I was going to Egypt, and that was that. I wasn't asked anything. I was extremely strictly brought up. I was supposed to be very unimportant. I had my orders and I took them. I couldn't argue with my mother. She became very irritable. I remember writing her letters then showing them to my father who would say, "Keep them for three days," and then, of course, I wouldn't send them. I mean, we were all right in the same house! She used to laugh a lot but she always struck me as being terribly selfish. She knew I loved animals and in the country I was allowed to have three dogs but when she was having a nap in the afternoon, she wouldn't have the dogs barking. Now, how can you stop dogs barking? How can you have puppies with none of them ever barking? So I used to practically *sit* on them while she was having this nap. Always this kind of element of "We mustn't irritate her whatever we do." She and my father used to have a lot of arguments which was very unpleasant. And I was sort of go-between, which made me extremely nervous. So the atmosphere, obviously, wasn't very happy.

'She was very proud of me and extremely jealous of me at the same time. And amazingly generous. She would give me the most beautiful clothes; spare me anything. But she couldn't understand me because I was a difficult person to understand. And she was jealous of my attachment to my father. He and I hardly ever had a quarrel.'

Margaret's mother's matriarchal role in the small family household was formidable. She was as unbending as Margaret, and while many children, especially girls who are spoilt by doting fathers, get away with murder, Margaret had no such chance under her mother's firm rule. She began to resent Helen and the power she brought to bear over her. In later years she, like her mother, was firm in her resolve and cultivated few, if any, lasting friendships with other women. Blood ran cold on the distaff side of the family.

And so the Whigham family set off to winter in Aswan. The Earl of Warwick, who was serving with the Grenadier Guards in Egypt, soon became aware of their arrival in Cairo and promptly sent Margaret an invitation to one of their dances. He fell in love with her at once and decided to leave on the same train as theirs for Aswan.

Margaret and Warwick spent all available time together over the next two months, he returning to Cairo after each weekend. She was thoroughly enjoying the romance in spite of her engagement to Aitken. 'I thought, well, Max and Fulke are a long, long way from each other, so they won't meet. So I just kept things as they were going for the moment. Fulke travelled back to London with us, from Egypt, and when I arrived I broke it off with Max. The press besieged us as the boat arrived because news had leaked out from Egypt and we were received with a great fanfare of trumpets when the boat docked.' Needless to say Whigham had cabled Charles Lyttle in London well in advance. The society heiress was to marry an earl.

'We took the Embassy Club for the night and had a big party to announce the engagement, and again, we had tremendous news coverage.'

There was also an unexpected surprise lying in store for her. She received information that was to cast a shadow over her hopes of continued happiness. An astrologer who was a guest at the club that night asked her birthdate and told her that people born under her sign on that day in the northern hemisphere would always be prone to treachery and prophesied that she was in danger of losing whatever good fortune and ambition she might have. The astrologer had failed to realize that she had inherited this treacherous trait from her father who had double-crossed the Celanese inventors to provide himself with his riches. Neither could she have foreseen that Margaret's deceitful nature would set in motion a train of events so overwhelming in their scope as to threaten the lives and happiness of many people who loved and respected her in the ensuing two decades.

After the excitement of the engagement had died down, Margaret's mother told her boldly that she had reservations about her forthcoming marriage: old Lady Warwick, Fulke's mother, Marjorie, had called on her to say, 'If you love your daughter, don't let her marry my son. He's a liar, he's ill-mannered, and he picks his nose.' 'And with that, my mother had a fit. But I must admit Fulke was off-hand and very rude. And then I was taken up to Warwick Castle to be introduced officially to Lady Warwick. We had already had the date set for the wedding by then at Westminster Abbey, the bridesmaids were chosen and I had chosen the design for my wedding dress.

'Then one day my father found Fulke lying on a sofa and he didn't get up when my father entered the room. What's more he didn't get up either when my mother went into the room, and that finished my father. He said to me, "You've got to break your engagement off to that young man. He's so rude *now*. What's he going to be like when you're married to him?" Besides which, instead of being charming and helpful to me while we were their guests at Warwick Castle, he neglected me, leaving me almost entirely to the mercy of the staff who were instructed to show me round. But I said, "It's too late, it's too late," for it had already been officially announced. And my father replied firmly, "It's *not* too late."

'And so I broke it off. Which was sad in a way because I think I did love him and my father gave me bad advice.'

However, according to Lady d'Avigdor-Goldsmid, whose bridesmaid Margaret was, there was another reason. She was well placed to know as a lifelong friend of Margaret's, and certainly one of her champions throughout. She asserts that Fulke was very relieved when Margaret broke off the engagement. When he came back to England from Egypt he realized that he really loved Rose Bingham, and wanted to marry her instead. Warwick married Rose Bingham a few months later and within five years accepted a contract from Metro-Goldwyn-Mayer who elevated him to movie stardom and reputedly paid him £2,000 a week with a built-in guarantee of a minimum £40,000 a year.

'Fulke was not a bad person,' Margaret said. 'I think he was as good as Charlie who, I must say, was always waiting in the background. Sweeny was terribly attractive so I began going round with him more. Fulke tried to get me back again but I wouldn't hear of it.'

And then she married Charlie.

CHAPTER THREE

Cupid and the Concierge

C HARLES Sweeny worked for his father's investment banking firm in London, Charterhouse Investment Trust. He spent much of his leisure time playing golf and became almost as good as his celebrated brother Robert, who had achieved championship status. Charles's pleasing personality appealed to Margaret, who had become increasingly attracted to handsome young men whose athleticism enabled them to weave their way round the bedroom as expertly as the ballroom. In physical appearance he was very like the young President John F. Kennedy with a clear, honest face, bright white teeth, heavenly blue eyes and healthy dark hair. His masculine Irish charm and charisma ensured that women swooned when he came into a room. He danced like a dream and he and Margaret embraced the dance floors of the Embassy and the 400 nightclubs until the early hours of the morning.

'I'd known Charlie ever since I was about sixteen when he was at Oxford and I was at Queen's Hill. He was Anglo-American, his father was Irish-American and although his grandfather had been very rich he lost the money. They were all terrific gamblers. There was a story in circulation that my future father-in-law had to leave America in a hurry and they ended up here, where they lived the rest of their lives never daring to go back to America – but they did, during the war, all the same.'

The young couple had arranged the date of their wedding but a setback presented itself: Sweeny was Catholic and Margaret Presbyterian. There was no alternative for her but to adopt the Catholic faith to marry the man she loved. 'I became Catholic after three months of very hard instruction. But I didn't become Catholic easily.

'I went to Colin Woodlock and we discussed and discussed and discussed until I said, "OK, I'll become a Catholic on two conditions." I think he thought I was mad, making bargains with the Faith. I told him that I wouldn't recognize the infallibility of the Pope because he'd only been infallible since 1886 and I wouldn't pray to a saint. I also said that if

I'm ever going to say a prayer, it's going to be to the Head Man. They accepted me on those two conditions because they seemed anxious to get the publicity it attracted. And it did get tremendous coverage. There was a great deal of ill-feeling over my becoming Catholic. I got a lot of nasty letters about it from both anti-Catholics – Church of England people – and Catholics themselves who thought me heathen for making a deal with the Church. Of course, it made headlines but I did it. It's strict and it's decisive, so then we married and I must say we were very happy and very much in love.'

The wedding took place on 21 February 1933 at the Brompton Oratory, where hordes of onlookers and press gasped at a wedding retinue to rival that of any English royalty. Margaret's wedding dress was the prototype for the one worn by Princess Elizabeth when she married the Duke of Edinburgh at Westminster Abbey fourteen years later. The design for it was repeated by Norman Hartnell.

'As Norman Hartnell had made so many of my clothes he was chosen to make my wedding dress. I remember the fittings at his showroom in Bruton Street, and how I let the press in to see my trousseau. As we were to be married at the Brompton Oratory which has a very long aisle, the train had to measure twenty-eight feet. The dress was in ivory satin and together with the train it was embroidered with orange blossom cut out of filigree lace and appliquéd with tiny pearls and silver-glass bugle beads. The veil was attached to my head by a narrow band of orange blossoms and I wore a string of pearls and a diamond bracelet. The bouquet consisted of arum lilies, roses and lilies-of-the-valley.

'We married in the very depth of the depression – and I remember my father saying, "You've chosen a very good moment to get married" – but we had tremendous presents despite the hard times people were going through. We had over two thousand presents all told.'

Nine bridesmaids, all Margaret's contemporaries, dressed in silver satin, were in attendance and admirers lined the street awaiting the wedding procession from the doors of the Oratory to Hyde Park Corner. The press turned out in force: 'Two thousand gate-crash the wedding. Crowds scrambled over pews to see Miss Margaret Whigham married,' the front page of the *Daily Mirror* led. 'Crowd's rush stops wedding procession. Women fight their way into church,' added the front page of another popular daily. 'Record queues of guests at Miss Whigham's wedding reception,' announced the *Daily Telegraph*.

The more sedate *Times* reported,

The bride's mother, in pale blue, entered with Mr Whigham soon after the stroke of eleven and they passed to their seats through an avenue of smiles and nods of recognition. The bridegroom and his best man, his brother Robert Sweeny, had taken their places at the front of the altar steps and, after several false alarms, the bridal group arrived and the organ pealed out an appropriate voluntary.

No sooner had the bridal procession moved up the aisle than the swing doors on either side of the main entrance were besieged by women who, using elbows and umbrellas freely, fought their way into the church, and for a moment stood swaying in a solid mass, completely cutting off the means of entry of guests who arrived late. The bride, leaning on her father's arm, set an example of graceful movement which her procession of nine bridesmaids nobly followed.

The six weeks' long honeymoon began in Paris and progressed to the West Indies on a cruise that took them to the north coast of America. On their return, however, Margaret was refused re-entry to Britain: she had lost her British status by having married an American and was therefore briefly a stateless, displaced person until the matter was resolved. Margaret and Charles had rented a house in Cadogan Place until they decided where to make their permanent home. She was expecting a baby when they returned from their honeymoon, which she lost, but within a few months she was pregnant again and, this time, became desperately ill. 'I was quite well at first but I got a cold and felt this terrible pain in my chest. It seemed like a lump but they said it was indigestion and that it would go away. But then I began to turn blue and they realized that I really was very ill. They found that my kidneys had gone to hell. Then I contracted double pneumonia. When you have it nowadays it means nothing but at that time there was no such thing as penicillin and they didn't have the antibiotics or the oxygen tents we have these days. Then I went into a coma and was taken to hospital. I vaguely remember tubes up my nose, which was all they had. It was oxygen. I was unconscious for a week and they gave me up for dead. All the most important doctors including Lord Dawson of Penn, the famous consultant, were summoned and simply said, "She cannot live. Her temperature's gone down way below normal. She's got infected kidneys and double pneumonia."'

The baby was stillborn.

'Everybody was there to say goodbye to me because they were convinced that I would die. "If only her temperature would rise," they said. But it wouldn't. It couldn't. Both our parents came and all sorts of other people. I must say, Charlie was distraught. He said that he refused to accept it or to believe it and went to get the priest round. Father Martindale came along and I can only just remember very, very hazily a figure at the end of my bed mumbling something. I was actually being given this extreme unction at the same time and within an hour or two my temperature began to rise. It really was a miracle. The hospital hadn't any explanation for it. They said the improvement in my illness had nothing to do with them. So I really was pleased to be Catholic. After that I was terribly ill for another four or five months. They were saying Masses for me all over England. I was getting water from Lourdes. There were crowds outside the hospital. Placards on every street corner read MARGARET WHIGHAM DYING. MARGARET DESPERATELY ILL.

'But Charlie wasn't very kind. He was going out to the Embassy every night in white-tie. Not with girls, necessarily, and there I was lying in hospital on the critical list, my child gone and feeling very weak and ill. He should have been there with me. My mother was furious and so was my nanny. I was given up for dead and the very moment they pronounced me out of danger, out he went to the Embassy Club that very night. I mean, it wasn't very cruel but it wasn't very kind either. I was very much in love with him. I'd only been married a year and I was miserable. I was crying half the night through and that wasn't helping much.

'And then they wanted me to go and convalesce abroad but I wouldn't go because I didn't want to leave him. So I went to Brighton with a nurse instead, which was pretty dreary. He used to come down for weekends but he wouldn't come down every bloody night. I mean, Brighton's only fifty minutes from London. I agree, he was working in London, but still, he could have come down every night to be with me. He was very selfish. And so I spent a month or so there in a home trying to get well.

'After I had recuperated I spent my entire time trying to catch up and had about eight miscarriages. All for various reasons. One, I was running after dogs, the other, I was in Vichy on the golf course watching Charlie play golf. It was no fun getting me home after that fiasco. I don't think it distressed Charlie as much as it distressed me. I was obsessed with it. I felt a complete failure as a woman aged twenty. Anyway, I had two healthy, very divine children in the end, Frances and Brian, and I would have liked to have more. Four, five, six. I loved having children. They're a great joy to have and whatever heartache they are, they're worth it.'

Having settled down to married life Charles Sweeny spent practically every weekend playing golf and although Margaret had always loathed the game and seldom watched her father play it, she followed Charles religiously and began to enjoy the tournaments. As her strength grew they wined and dined at the best places in London and Paris and captured the British imagination for romanticism and glamour in the Vivien Leigh–Laurence Olivier tradition. They enjoyed visiting the cinema and listening to the popular music of the day. Their favourite composer was Cole Porter who, in one of his most often played and sung songs, 'You're the Tops', immortalized Margaret in the lyrics.

After two years they decided to buy a home of their own and found a house: 6 Sussex Gardens, in Bayswater. Although the district nowadays has acquired a somewhat sleazy reputation for ladies of the night and layabouts, it was extremely fashionable in the thirties, despite being on 'the other side of the park' from Belgravia. The house was a stone's throw from Hyde Park, through which a casual walk brought them to Kensington Gardens. One of their closest neighbours was Barbara Hutton, Margaret's child-hood friend, who lived round the corner in Hyde Park Gardens with her latest husband, Count Reventlow, and whom they visited frequently.

Decorating and furnishing the house became enjoyable chores for Margaret: while Charles spent the day at the office she passed her time in choosing the décor and simple modern furniture of the period. They had a Rolls-Royce and chauffeur, provided by Margaret's father since Charles's salary was no more than any other young banker. 'There were no money problems,' Margaret remembered. 'Of course, both the families were behind us. My father paid for my illness, for instance. It was long and costly. But Charlie always worked. That I will say. He was at the office every day. He was never idle.'

Charles, however, was excessively possessive and had a quick Irish temper. He forbade Margaret to go out socially without him, no matter the size of the party, and she was certainly not permitted to dance with other men. They entertained mainly at home and acquired an entirely different, settled lifestyle. Although not prone to give much time to charity work, Margaret accepted the chairmanship of the London Society for Teaching and Training of the Blind Fund and volunteered to sell out the première of the new film *Beloved Enemy*, which starred Merle Oberon, to raise funds. She filled the house, making £1,500 for the charity, but on the day of the première her husband's secretary telephoned to say that he had been taken ill and was rushed to hospital. He could not attend. Margaret contacted the doctor who reported that Charles had a perforated stomach ulcer and an immediate operation was necessary to save his life. He had suffered from an incipient duodenal ulcer for some time, caused by stress, overwork and inattention to a balanced diet.

When he came home a holiday was deemed essential for him to recuperate and Charles and Margaret decided on a visit to America, where Margaret hadn't set foot since the age of fourteen. They set sail on the *Île de France* and arrived in New York where they were entertained with customary American warmth and hospitality. Their first invitation was to attend the opening of a new nightclub called the Monte

Carlo run by Fefe Ferry, who led a troupe of beautiful dancers billed as Les Girls. They travelled on to Palm Beach, Florida, and there enjoyed the luxury and opulence of the community at the invitation of 'Laddie' Sanford, the polo player, and his wife Mary, before setting off for Hialeah, Miami, as guests of Mrs Woolworth Donahue, Barbara Hutton's aunt, who sent along her private air-conditioned coach complete with bathroom fittings made of solid gold to collect them.

On their visit to the Hialeah racecourse, while they were sweltering in temperatures up to 100°F in the shade, Margaret received a message from the world-renowned beautician Elizabeth Arden asking how she kept her skin and complexion so cool. 'By using Elizabeth Arden make-up,' was her reply, after which she was invited to dine with Miss Arden in her Fifth Avenue apartment in New York.

Soon after their return to England their old friend Douglas Fairbanks Snr invited Charles and Margaret to join him and his wife Sylvia for a short stay in Monte Carlo which they accepted enthusiastically.

After several more miscarriages, Margaret's first child, Frances, was born in June 1937 at Marylebone's Beaumont House nursing home. Her happiness seemed cemented, and for the time being at least, her personal good fortune continued when, two years later in 1939, while she and

Charles were staying once more with Douglas Fairbanks in Monte Carlo, Margaret found herself pregnant again. It was during their stay that war broke out, making their return to England essential. It was a difficult journey but they managed it safely, and Margaret spent the winter months of pregnancy at her parents-in-law's rented house near Worthing, returning to London in March the following year.

'Brian was born in April 1940 in the middle of the phoney war, when nothing was happening. I gave birth to him on the day that Norway was invaded. There were an awful lot of air-raid alarms in London and we didn't realize what was going to happen. We thought we were going to be invaded so Charlie decided that we had to close the house. It was too dangerous to have a baby there so I had Brian at the Dorchester Hotel which was the only building that had concrete in it. It was a divine way to have a baby, in a hotel.

'The American Ambassador Joseph Kennedy was quite a good friend of ours and we used to go down to his house in Sunningdale every single night. He said to me, "Get out of England, Margaret. This country's finished." I was absolutely horrified at him saying this. Of course, I was married to an American and they kept on sending ships over for us and every time the ship came I was upset because I didn't know what the hell to do with the children who were half

American. It was all very worrying and I wished to God they wouldn't send any more ships. And then my father said that if I went to America or sent the children there he would never speak to me again, so *that* finished *that*. He settled the argument for me and I felt very relieved because I didn't want to go at all.'

The truth was, though, that Margaret might well have enjoyed having children but she didn't want to be burdened with them. Quite frankly, they were spoiling her fun. She had no true maternal instincts but she would never admit that they hampered her social life. They were not neglected, of course, and Margaret justified her dispersal of them in the firm belief that they were perfectly well looked after by their nanny and were in good hands. Her children fulfilled the same role as that of her toys. They became substitutes for her teddies. Just as she had been at their age, they were well cared for by others than their parents.

'Then we sent the children up to the Aberconways' house in North Wales, as far away as possible from the east coast because we thought that's where the Germans would invade. The bombs began to drop and Charlie said that I *had* to get out of London and join the children and I kept saying, "I'm not going, I'm not going." Then there was a terrible night when the glass blew in and black smoke filled the room. "Look, it's happening!" he called, and I said that I didn't care. I didn't want to go but he persisted and made me go to the children. Frances was three years old and Brian was only two months by then.

'He got me to Euston station and as I was waiting for the train a bomb hit Euston! I said, "Look, you're getting me killed. You've brought me to this station to get me killed!" And then I got on the train which was packed with refugees who were going to Liverpool. There were goats, there were children, there was everything. And I sat in the carriage crying. Crying with rage. A very nice businessman patted me on the knee and said pacifyingly, "Never mind, you'll soon be out of London," and I blubbered, "That's what I'm crying about! I don't want to leave London!" I cried all the way up to the Aberconways' which is beyond Bangor in North Wales. It took us three hours to get there and when I got to the station I thought, I'm not staying here *one* night. And the first night there, I saw Lady Aberconway coming down the stairway with a candle, like Lady Macbeth, and that really did it. The *gloom*!

'By this time, aside from the two children, I had a nanny and a nurserymaid, so it was quite a party. So I sent myself a telegram which arrived very quickly, to say that Charlie was very ill and I had to go back straight away. And I took the train back feeling triumphant. Beaming! Beaming. Everybody was lying at the bottom of the carriage looking miserable and I was beaming! They must have thought I was mad.

'When I got back, Charlie said, "I give up. I give up."

'Then September came and the war really began. We had all the American Service over here. We had General Arnold, General Cheyney, the lot. To begin with America wasn't in the war. It was only the Canadian Allied Forces at this time.'

After Margaret's return from Wales she and Charles moved into the comparative safety of the newly built Dorchester Hotel in Park Lane, where they lived for the next five years until the end of the war. They believed that its basement would provide adequate shelter from the welter of bombs.

In 1940 Margaret joined the Beaver Club where she worked as a waitress. This was where she first met Churchill's daughter-in-law Pamela, who later married Averell Harriman. The two were to remain great friends. It was a forces canteen near Admiralty Arch but working long hours so soon after her son's birth proved too much of a strain and she was transferred to the Royal Air Force Benevolent Fund where she remained until the bombing of Pearl Harbor brought the United States into the war.

'We were naturally all thankful when America came into the war, I can tell you, we were all praying for success at Pearl Harbor. And I joined the American Red Cross straight away. I was the second woman to wear an American Red Cross uniform in England. I was under Mrs Anthony Biddle whose husband was ambassador to about eight different countries and she was not only a rich woman but she had great power. She ran a club for women officers, and we had the best restaurant in the whole of London. I was put in charge of entertainment and we had a show every Thursday night. I had to get very big-named stars such as Bob Hope, Jack Buchanan or Florence Desmond to entertain everybody. Bing Crosby and Marlene Dietrich were kind enough to come along too.

'We had a frightfully pretty uniform. It was Air Force blue, with a red-lined coat and a white shirt or white jersey and plain white stockings. I had mine made at Molyneux. I saw Margaret Biddle wearing her pearls with her white sweater one day, so I thought I would wear my pearls with my white sweater too. I thought I looked pretty nifty in this uniform and got Dorothy Wilding to take photographs of me. But she put one of the photographs of me in her display window, and one day Harvey Gibson, who was Head of the American Red Cross, came over and said, "Who the hell is that woman in the photograph I've just seen in an American uniform wearing pearls?" So both Margaret and I were told to take our pearls off.'

Dorothy Wilding was a superlative society photographer for several decades. She was one of the few women to attain acclaim in this male-dominated domain at that time. Her studio studies of the famous ranked in the class of Sir Cecil Beaton, Horst and Hoyningen-Huene.

'It was all tremendously gay, and great fun and very

dangerous. We were on twenty-four-hour alert all day and every day. At that time you always carried your tin helmet with you. You never knew what was going to come and hit you. And, as everybody else did, I got very close to bombs falling.

'I remember once, there was a man who was the head of Paramount, David Rose. He wasn't the famous musician who had composed 'The Stripper' and so forth, this was another man. He used to have private film shows for his guests, and once he had one called *Road to Morocco*, and he had General Eisenhower, General Bradley and all the American top brass there. And when they saw this thing come on, they nearly had seizures, because it was on the eve of the landing in Algiers and they thought David Rose knew something. They all rushed out of the theatre whispering, "There's been a leak. There's been a leak." But he hadn't a clue. It was Dorothy Lamour, Bing Crosby and Bob Hope in a film. No more, no less.

'As for Charlie, he was never well. He always had ulcers and just wouldn't do any good on a front line. If you're on the front line and you have ulcers, one meal and you're home again. So he couldn't enlist. But he formed the Eagle Squadron as his contribution to the war effort. It consisted of the American boys who volunteered to come over here to fight, long before America came into the war. They came from everywhere, Utah, Texas, California, the lot, and they joined the Royal Air Force as the Eagle Squadron. And *he* started the whole thing. Sir Archibald Sinclair, who was in power then, was instrumental in having an Act of Parliament changed so that they wouldn't have to take an oath of allegiance to the King because they were American citizens. Charlie also formed a Home Guard of all the Americans who couldn't fight because we needed every man we had.'

In spite of bombs dropping on London the only mishap Margaret suffered was on a visit to her chiropodist in Bond Street in 1945. His practice was on the first floor and as she left she opened the lift door and promptly fell forty feet to the base of the shaft. She fell on her side, badly damaging her back. She lay there groaning with pain, fearful that the lift would descend from an upper floor where it had lodged, crushing her to death, but the porter had heard her calls and went to her rescue. Margaret was rushed to the nearby St George's Hospital at Hyde Park Corner (now an exclusive hotel). They found that she had not broken her back but needed thirty stitches to her head and doctors predicted that she would need to remain in hospital for at least three months. Typically, Margaret was out within three weeks, although she felt desperately weak for a while and lost the senses of taste and smell for the next four years.

By this time, Margaret had become aware that Charlie

was being unfaithful to her and their marriage began to show signs of strain. 'We led a young married life, going round with young married people,' Margaret said. 'Very respectable. I didn't ever go out with anybody but Charlie. Never, never, never. I mean, I was being a model wife all the time, *which is quite ironic, isn't it?*' All that changed when Charlie found his satisfaction elsewhere and she found male companions with whom she dined and danced at the 400 Club. The husband who had always been so strict about Margaret's going out at night without him at her side became indifferent to her movements and they saw little of one another except over weekends. Margaret might be described as one of the first feminists. When she discovered Charles's adultery, she dismissed the constraints of her Catholic marriage and took up the same pastime. It was a courageous step, but the love she had felt for Charles had gone. It had, in any case, been purely physical, and when that went by the board, there was nothing to replace it. Margaret seemed neither heartbroken nor disappointed: she knew that there were plenty of men to entrance. She also believed implicitly in self-preservation and when she saw warning lights, always moved on. She was not yet thirty years old, and her life lay ahead of her. She was soon to be seen dining and dancing with Group Captain Max Aitken, the man to whom she had become engaged thirteen years before, and attending a film première with the American Colonel Hammond. Margaret and Charles accepted that their marriage was basically over; she accused him of having secret affairs with other women and he was convinced of her infidelity too. Although friends advised her to arrange a quick break from her marriage she decided to wait until after the war, while Charles, as a Roman Catholic, was adamantly against entertaining the prospect of either divorce or a complicated annulment.

When the war ended in 1945 Margaret decided on a trial separation. The best way to achieve this was to visit America where she had visions of starting a new life. Her spirits, however, were dampened when she realized that it was almost impossible to get a passage across the Atlantic. Every available berth was booked for essential traffic only. Margaret explored every avenue in her determination to escape and found that she had two alternatives: she could go either as a GI bride on a liner sharing a cabin with three other women and possibly their children, or could travel on a banana boat with a cabin to herself. She chose the latter, concerned that she would be the only woman on board among twenty-five male passengers. Although this in itself was a little daunting, Margaret had no idea of the discomfort she would endure on the voyage, having travelled first class all her life.

As she kissed her father goodbye she kissed goodbye too

to the marriage that seemed to have been made in heaven, and accepted the risk of losing her two young children, in what could become a bitter battle for their custody. The boat departed from Tilbury Docks in Essex and sailed east through the Thames estuary then round the south of England into the Channel before heading west.

But this was insignificant compared to the trepidation she felt for an uncertain future.

The ten-day trip on the stormy sea reflected the state of her marriage and proved the most tormenting time of her life so far. It took five days to reach the Channel and her fellow passengers were a far cry from the lively company to which she was accustomed. Her reception in New York, though, more than compensated for the turbulent crossing. She was received on the dock by an old acquaintance, Admiral Luis de Florez who, accompanied by two aides, two cars and a naval lorry for her travelling trunks, escorted her to the luxurious hotel where she stayed for the first few days of her three-month visit. The rest of her time was spent as guest of her uncle, Jim Whigham, who had retired from his journalistic jaunts and who whiled away his time on the golf course.

Determined to enjoy her holiday to the full Margaret accepted a string of invitations from eligible bachelors including Count Serge Obolensky. They were often to be seen holding one another very close on the intimate El Morocco dance floor. Similar amorous attentions were displayed by the Belgian-born John Truyons, who became her constant companion in New York. As a married society beauty seen so often in the company of single men, Margaret's behaviour set tongues wagging and fuelled rumours of her intended divorce. She also caught up with several high-ranking naval officers at parties, who had become friends since the days of the Beaver Club.

On Margaret's return to England in the summer her first social outing during the season without her husband took place at Sutton Place in Surrey. The occasion was a ball given by the Duchess of Sutherland who subsequently sold the house to Margaret's lifelong friend, the American multi-millionaire J. Paul Getty.

It was at the next important function, a party given by the Honourable Lady Olive Baillie, that she renewed her acquaintance with the beautiful British film actress Diana Napier, wife of the celebrated Austrian tenor Richard Tauber. Lady Baillie, whose friends rivalled Nancy Astor's 'Cliveden Set', was chatelaine of the elegant little Leeds Castle near Maidstone in Kent, one of the oldest inhabited castles in Britain, complete with an immaculate moat afloat with white swans, the gardens enlivened by her pet parrots and other exotic birds. Lady Baillie had invited Margaret to the reception of her daughter Susan Winn's marriage to Lord Ampthill's eldest son.

Diana Napier and Margaret had met when they were

both living at the Dorchester during the war years. Diana's role for the war effort was as a FANY – in the First Aid Nursing Yeomanry, formed during the First World War, when it consisted of mounted nurses – working with the Poles.

The Sweenys and the Taubers had been friends of Lady Baillie for some time and had spent many weekends together at Leeds Castle. Tauber, however, had been living more or less openly with his mistress Esther Moncrieff at Park West, the block of flats near Marble Arch, but died two years after the end of the war aged fifty-eight of lung cancer. Diana remarried after his death and she and Margaret remained friends until Margaret asked Diana for help when her marriage to the Duke of Argyll began to fail.

Since her return from America Margaret had been an ideal mother and had taken Frances and Brian to Switzerland. After the holiday, Charles agreed to their divorce – much against his will – which was granted on grounds of constructive desertion. It became final in 1947, the following year. Now morally and legally liberated Margaret paid another visit to America, this time crossing the Atlantic on the luxury liner *Queen Elizabeth* in the manner to which she had always been accustomed.

Margaret's parents had sold the Ascot house and bought a sumptuous Queen Anne house in Mayfair's Upper Grosvenor Street. Helen, however, now crippled with arthritis could no longer manage the stairs and they took up permanent residence at the Dorchester until she died, at over eighty, in 1955. Margaret's father made over the house to her, valued at £100,000. (It sold for more than £2.5 million less than fifty years later.) She moved in on her return from America and began entertaining alone on a lavish scale.

'I had a really wonderful time from the period between forty-three and fifty-one. I had a ball! I had this house, I had children. I had money. I could ask whoever I wanted. Charlie was always so orthodox and boring. That's when I began entertaining. Nobody had so much fun as I had in those eight years. Nobody. Nobody. The house was always filled, packed with the most amusing people, sometimes with eighteen to dinner with another ten joining us afterwards. I didn't go on travelling as much then because I had the children growing up and I had Frances with me all the time. She never went to boarding school. Ever. She was with me every day of the week.'

The house, which occupied three floors, backed on to an immaculate garden reaching to a five-roomed cottage, a garage and chauffeur's quarters leading to the mews.

'There wasn't anybody in the political, theatrical, Hollywood or social world who I either didn't know or hadn't met,' Margaret said. 'It wasn't just *Debrett*, I had a tremendously wide range of friends not just the boring aristocracy.'

One man, however, was not among the usual circle of

suitors: she met him on a train returning to London from a trip to Paris. Margaret had been staying at the Ritz on a shopping spree in 1947 and asked the concierge to book her a seat on the Golden Arrow. The stranger had travelled up to Paris from his house in Biarritz in south-west France, stayed the night in his club and the following morning wandered over to the Ritz where he, too, asked the concierge to book him a seat on the Golden Arrow to London. Margaret and he found themselves seated opposite one another. He remembered that she was the beautiful young woman he had seen descending the famous staircase at the Café de Paris in London before the war when he had misguidedly remarked to his then wife, the Hon. Janet Aitken, that that captivating creature was the woman he would marry one day. During their pleasant exchanges on the train he explained that he had been following her progress through press accounts and reports from friends and was, indeed, sorry to learn that she had recently divorced Charles Sweeny.

Margaret found her travelling companion, Captain Ian Douglas Campbell, intelligent and attractive but he appeared somewhat distant. He had left a prisoner-of-war camp the year before and found his freedom strange and bewildering.

'He was prisoner-of-war in Germany on the border of Poland,' Margaret said, explaining that he had spent the entire war years in the camp. 'He was taken in nineteen forty, I think, to Rommel. It was when the whole 81st Division were all taken in a bag. It was an awful misjudgement of Churchill's. He kept thinking the French would save them, but when they didn't do so, they were just captured. There were a great many men in the Division.'

Ian Campbell married twice for money. He had none, but he was attractive, virile and aristocratic. Imprisoned and deprived of women's company for five years, Campbell set about making up for lost time. Margaret, too, as a highly sexed woman whose instincts had been suppressed by convention rather than choice, yearned for physical contact. They knew instinctively that they could, and would, satisfy each other's sexual needs. On their arrival in London they went to her Mayfair home supposedly for a drink…

The next time they met was again in Paris, at an American friend's party. Although Margaret was a divorcée, and therefore free to associate with whom she liked, social mores were not as relaxed as they are now: every move she made had to be taken with care. Her name and her face were well known in society and to the press. By the same token, Campbell was a respectably married man with two children.

Margaret had carefully orchestrated their clandestine meeting in Paris, and both were pleased to see each other again – she, perhaps, more so because she had discovered not only that he was unhappy in his marriage but, through the death of a male cousin, he had recently succeeded to an illustrious title and had become Duke of Argyll.

Among her distinguished entourage Margaret courted Baron Alexis de Redé, an old friend of the Chilean millionaire Arturo Lopez. On 13 January 1950 she arranged a luncheon at home for him. As she needed another man to make up the numbers, she invited the Duke of Argyll. He willingly accepted, and the die was cast.

Ian was lazy, broke and had expensive tastes befitting his station.

Margaret was rich, desirable, available and, with her father's millions to back her up, she was capable of buying anything she wanted. The chance of becoming a duchess was now within her range, and the trappings of that role acted as a potent aphrodisiac. She set her cap at Argyll with undaunting determination. He in turn was captivated by the attentions of the charming and much sought-after society favourite. They were often seen together doing the rounds of West End theatres and attending social gatherings, but they needed to secure his divorce if they were to contemplate marriage.

The Duke's second wife was a rich socialite, Louise Clews, daughter of the American sculptor Henry Clews and former wife of the Hon. Andrew Vanneck, brother of the 5th Baron Huntingfield. Her grandfather had 'founded' Wall Street. Louise refused the Duke a divorce and the lovers had no alternative but to play a waiting game. More significantly, Louise and the Duke had two sons, his heirs, to whom Louise became trustee.

On 25 March 1950, and again in Paris, the Duke announced to the press that he had located the *Duq Florencia*, a Spanish Armada galleon which had sunk off Tobermory, Isle of Mull, in 1588. He was its hereditary owner, his ancestors having been granted salvage rights by James I. Several efforts had been made to get at the treasure, with an estimated value of £30,000,000, which, according to local legend, had been aboard the vessel. The ship also carried a crown, sent by the Pope, with which Spanish forces had proposed to crown a Roman Catholic king of England. Royal Navy divers reported that they had found the galleon, and suction pumps brought up two ancient medallions. Before access could be gained to the treasure, though, about 20,000 tons of silt had to be removed.

Spurred on by the news of his treasure trove, Margaret needed a subterfuge to see the Duke again. She accepted an invitation to attend her old friend Barbara Hutton's ball in Paris and asked him to escort her. He readily agreed and together they attended the glittering ball where the Maharajah and Maharanee of Jaipur were guests of honour. A week later they went to the Travellers' Club ball, also in Paris, at which the Duke and Duchess of Windsor held court. Notables congregated from all corners: Cornelia

Grey and Norman Winston from America, the Jaipurs once more and the Marquis de Cuevas from Monte Carlo.

Towards the end of the month the Duke received shattering news: his eighteenth-century ancestral home, Inveraray Castle, was ablaze: flames had shot through the roof of the east wing where the staff slept. Falling timbers had roused his secretary, Miss Clegg, who ran through the wing rousing the staff and summoning the fire brigade. Although the damage was extensive, the museum, which included relics from the Tobermory galleon, was unharmed. The Duke left Paris immediately to inspect the damage. He asked Margaret to accompany him to Scotland, which she did with unashamed enthusiasm.

The London season was in full swing and although until now the Duke and Margaret had limited their public appearances to places and events outside the confines of London society they grew more courageous as the season progressed. First they were seen together at the Duchess of Sutherland's annual ball and later at the coming-out party at Quaglino's of the banker Henry Tiarks's daughter, Henrietta, who became débutante of the season and subsequently married the Marquess of Tavistock, heir to the Duke of Bedford. Argyll and Margaret next appeared arm in arm at the 51st Highland Division Ball at Gleneagles in Scotland, and their intentions were made abundantly clear when he took her up to Inveraray Castle again in October where they spent a month together.

The Duke honourably promised to marry Margaret as soon as he had divorced his wife. He proposed to her in a box at the West End theatre where they had attended a performance of Jean Anouilh's romantic play, *Ring Round the Moon*. In hindsight, the plot, which concerns a twin's attempt to rescue his brother from what he believes will be a disastrous marriage, seems to parallel Margaret and the Duke's eventual union, except that Argyll had not been forewarned of impending peril in his intended partnership. The audience left the theatre at the end of the performance but the door to the Argyll box had jammed, locking him and Margaret inside, and he seized his opportunity. She agreed to become his third wife without hesitation.

The Duke's second wife, Louise, divorced him on the grounds of his adultery. In society at that time it was customary for the husband always to allow his wife to divorce him on grounds of adultery, no matter what the real circumstances surrounding the divorce may have been. It was a gentleman's duty to protect the reputation of his wife. However, this divorce was a very different and scandalous affair. During the hearing at the Edinburgh Court of Session, Louise produced evidence of her husband's adultery from an entry in the register of a Crowborough, Sussex, hotel. It was signed 'Mr and Mrs Campbell' and Louise proved that it was her husband's handwriting. Much

against her will the second Duchess was granted her freedom but gained custody of their two sons, the elder of
whom was heir to the dukedom of Argyll and Inveraray
Castle. Neither parent had the independent financial means
of supporting them so Margaret offered £1,000 a year
for five years for their education and this was gratefully
received.

Within six hours of the Duke's divorce becoming final,
wearing a soft grey chiffon day-dress, a tiny lime-yellow
feathered hat and carrying a bouquet of orchids, Margaret
became the Duchess of Argyll on 22 March 1951 when they
married at Caxton Hall.

In so doing she had neatly slipped her elegant neck into
a noose knotted by herself.

CHAPTER FOUR

The Campbells Are Coming

T HE grand old Duke of Argyll, tenth in his line and the cousin from whom Ian inherited the title and estates of Inveraray, was the eccentric, forthright and respected chief of the Campbell clan, the largest and oldest in the Highlands. Niall Diarmid Campbell, who died at the age of seventy-seven, became affectionately known as Neil Duke, the holder of nineteen titles, some of which dated back to the fourteenth century. He was a stickler for ancient rights and when in 1922 the Officer of Works proposed repairing Dunstaffnage Castle of which he was Keeper he threatened to clap into the dungeon any official attempting to carry out the project.

The son of a banker, he succeeded to the dukedom in 1914 on the death of his uncle, who left £600,000 together with the estates that stretched for more than 150,000 acres across the Western Highlands. After serving in the First World War with the Argyll and Sutherland Highlanders, the bachelor Duke returned to Inveraray where he refused to install many modern inventions. He had neither heating nor wireless and only reluctantly put electric light in his bedroom to make reading in bed more comfortable. He never owned a motor car and could be seen riding round the countryside on a bicycle, dressed in his kilt from which he was seldom separated. At the age of sixty-six he took off his coat and wheeled barrow-loads of stones and carried hods of bricks over several days to repair the church of Inveraray.

Before him, the ninth Duke, an only son, succeeded his father in 1900. He had married HRH The Princess Louise, Queen Victoria's fourth daughter, in 1871. She was somewhat Bohemian and became a sculptress. The match produced no children and the Princess died in 1939 at the age of ninety-one.

The eleventh Duke was born in Paris in 1903 with American and French blood as well as Scots. In 1899 his father, Douglas Walter Campbell, nephew of the ninth Duke, married Aimée Lawrence, who came of an old New York family on her father's side and a French one on her mother's. They settled in Paris where young Ian was brought up and learnt to speak fluent French. He was sent to England in 1913 where his schooling began at Eton and ended at Oxford. He became heir-presumptive to the dukedom of Argyll at the age of twenty-two on the death of his father, who left him only £15,000. As he had acquired no skills and had no professional leanings he was unable to earn a living and offered his services to the Conservative Central Office after settling down to live at White's, his London club. Five years later he married the heiress Janet Aitken and proceeded to raise much-needed cash to stave off his creditors by pawning her jewellery *en route* to their honeymoon destination, which her father, Lord Beaverbrook, proceeded to buy back.

Still hard-up, and worse off than ever since the Wall Street crash, Ian was rescued by Beaverbrook, who offered him work as a journalist on one of his newspapers. This, however, proved difficult since the family had gone to live in a villa outside Cannes shortly before the South of France became a fashionable winter resort. Ian squandered over £200,000 in sixteen years and found his marriage on the rocks. After his divorce from Janet, he married an American, Mrs Louise Clews Vanneck, whom he had known for several years. It is clear that he married her for her money. In order to recover financially and to get his new marriage on a firm footing Ian borrowed £30,000 against his rights of inheritance to Inveraray Castle and after travelling widely in Europe he and Louise made their home in France.

Louise gave birth to Ian's son and heir, Ian, Marquess of Lorne, in 1937, and to their second son, Lord Colin Campbell, in 1946. Colin married Georgie Ziadie, born in Kingston, Jamaica, within four days of their first meeting and they were divorced under a year later. Although she had been brought up as a boy until she was fourteen, a 'minor operation' was rumoured to have confirmed Georgie's womanhood. She adopted the name Lady Colin Campbell in preference to the more correct Georgie, Lady Colin Campbell, after the dissolution of their marriage in 1975. She became a close friend of Margaret, united by their feelings for their former Campbell husbands. During the early nineties she wrote salacious books about the English royal family. After Colin's birth Ian and Louise grew apart, but they decided to stay in France and bought a villa known as Kittera, in Biarritz. It was from here, in 1947, that Ian took the trip that changed the course of his life. He left Biarritz for London, flying first to Paris and then boarding the Golden Arrow, where he discovered the beautiful ex-Mrs Charles Sweeny seated opposite him.

On becoming Duke of Argyll, Ian also became Chief of the Clan Campbell worldwide, Hereditary Master of the Royal Household in Scotland, Keeper of the Great Seal of Scotland, and the castles of Dunoon, Dunstaffnage, Tarbert and Carrick, and Deputy Lieutenant of Argyllshire in 1950. However, he was faced with mammoth death duties, together with the costs of restoring Inveraray Castle. Dry rot had developed over a hundred years of neglect while fire damage to the roof of the east wing and rot in other roof areas rendered the eighty-eight-roomed building practically uninhabitable. His hopes of scooping up a fortune with the salvaging of the sunken galleon in Tobermory Bay now seemed bleak since he was unable to realize the estimated £15,000 cost of raising the vessel.

Ian knew how keen Margaret was to become his wife and he began to cultivate her. He was aware that as well as being heir to her multi-millionaire father she also had taste, style, a position in society and an illustrious international circle of friends. She lacked only one thing – which he could provide: a title. Ian put a price on making Margaret his Duchess, and she, sorely tempted to elevate herself to the aristocracy, took her father to see the castle and to meet her intended. He was impressed with what he saw: pictures by Reynolds and Gainsborough, magnificent pieces of ancient silver, fine eighteenth-century French gilt furniture, Beauvais tapestries, Sèvres and Meissen porcelain and other treasures too numerous to list.

Whigham agreed to advance a substantial sum for the restoration and rehabilitation of the castle, in return for the assurance that his daughter's marriage was guaranteed and that she would be maintained in the comfort to which she was accustomed. Alas, however, as an astute Scots businessman, Whigham wanted tangible value for his money: instead of paying up in the form of a dowry, in return for his financing of the project Ian was to make over to Margaret under a Deed of Gift certain chattels such as paintings as security. This, Ian willingly agreed to. However, the entire estate had been placed in trust over which he had no control without the agreement of the trustees. Nevertheless, he signed the documents proffered by Whigham and the couple were married shortly afterwards.

'We poured a great deal of money into the castle,' Margaret volunteered, 'but my father never said a word about it. Nor did I. Because Ian was a very difficult man. You've got to keep a man's ego and pride. Besides, it's not an attractive thing to talk about. The castle was about to have all its roofs taken off because under Scottish law you don't have to pay rates on a property without a roof. Ian hadn't a *bean*. Not a penny to his name.'

And so the debt-ridden Duke and his rich new wife arrived at Inveraray Castle for their honeymoon in the spring of 1951 where Donald MacArthur, the Duke's own piper, led the newly-weds through the castle grounds. The Duke, heavily kilted, sporran in position, marched behind with Margaret clutching her wedding bouquet and looking anxious – as she may well have been when the Duke swept her into his arms to carry her over the historic threshold of their future stronghold and nearly dropped her. They were greeted by the tenants, the townspeople, and the following morning they got down to making the castle habitable. Margaret spent the first three weeks of her marriage in the basement searching for china and glass. She discovered that while she and Ian were using Woolworths plates and tumblers, the staff were unwittingly using Crown Derby and Waterford. She soon made a change in that state of affairs.

Meals were prepared in a gigantic old-fashioned stone-floored kitchen by the devoted old cook, and the retainer butler, Alec Dingle, struggled along endless stone passages and staircases to serve hot meals to Their Graces, who were exhausted after a day spent unpacking the treasures of the rain-drenched castle where buckets had been placed at strategic points in the hall to catch the pouring rain.

The society hostess who had seldom entered her own kitchen in Mayfair, whose face and hands were daily treated by Elizabeth Arden in Bond Street, who could neither cook nor sew, had, however, had the tenacity to buy half a dozen overalls and serviceable gloves and secured the support of eight of the estate workers from nine till five in sorting out the trash from the treasures accumulated over the years.

The honeymoon coincided with the planned start of the search for the Tobermory treasure. Once again, Ian had to approach his new wife and her father for finance.

Once again, they paid up – and also to keep Ian's two sons in schools appropriate to their station. Once they had established themselves with staff, locals, trustees and finance Ian and Margaret set off for Spain on their official honeymoon, taking in Paris on the way.

The trustees of the estate were sceptical about the new Duke's ability to administer the property, particularly since he hadn't visited the castle for over twenty years and had appeared to them to have no interest in its viability as a business concern. They also considered him a foreigner since he was half French and had lived abroad for so long. Similarly, they had their reservations about the new Duchess whose reputation was far removed from either country or Scottish life. She did not hesitate to remind them that she at least was 100 per cent Scots.

Later in 1951, however, the trustees of the Argyll estate were obliged to sell off the island of Tiree, known for centuries as the 'Granary of the Hebrides', to meet death duties. Consisting of about 20,270 acres, Tiree, situated in the Inner Hebrides, fifteen miles west of Mull, was said to boast the best snipe shooting in Europe. Also up for sale was part of the Argyll estate in Inveraray and letters were sent to the local shopkeepers offering them the opportunity of buying the premises they had hitherto rented. A number of farms in Kintyre were sold for the same reason.

Once they had settled back in Britain, Ian told Margaret that since she would be spending so much time with him at Inveraray Castle in the future it hardly seemed worthwhile keeping on her London home. But Margaret declared that she had no intention of disposing of her sumptuous Mayfair establishment, fully equipped with cook, butler, maid and chauffeur and all the trimmings that accompanied her lust for London life, but that she would spend as much time with him in Scotland as possible. (As time would prove, this was not conducive to a happy life for a newly married couple.) Margaret was well aware that she would have no control over the administration of the castle whereas she was in charge of her own home.

Geographically, Inveraray and Mayfair were too far apart for frequent short visits and had she had the wisdom to acquire, in addition to her Mayfair home, a country house perhaps in Kent, Sussex, Surrey or the fashionable Cotswolds where the English aristocracy and royalty flocked, she might have enjoyed weekends and the autumns there and kept out of trouble. Instead, she was let loose on the few society people remaining in London who were as bored and at a loose end as she was. Although the Duke enjoyed the countryside and his newly acquired Inveraray Castle, Margaret hated it. She disliked mud and had no time for country folk or the lives they led. At the end of the London season around the Glorious Twelfth of August she escaped to Europe, Morocco or Egypt just as her London friends took to the country after the royals had departed for Balmoral, and Parliament was in recess.

At Inveraray Margaret's activities were not confined to the castle: the town consisted of a population of five hundred people who relied on a mobile cinema for occasional entertainment, so a decision was taken to provide the townsfolk with a picture-house. It was Margaret who, with enterprise and initiative, converted the drill hall. The town leaders were called to a meeting at the castle and told that the drill hall would be made available for six months initially, equipped as a cinema and films hired from London. Margaret offered to guarantee any financial loss if it failed but if it succeeded it would become the town's property. They agreed. Margaret borrowed tapestries and curtains from the castle to decorate the interior, sent the castle's master-joiner to build a platform and enlisted the head gardener to supply flowers to place beneath the screen. The new two-hundred-seater cinema soon began to attract audiences and to show a profit with a programme of four film shows a week. As a further contribution to the community, Margaret also paid for repairs to the defunct old public clock and rehung it in the church tower. A project to restore and repaint the Georgian houses in the town was curtailed, however, because of the £100,000 in estimated costs. The work was finally done several years later with the help of a government subsidy.

Signs of strain in the Argyll marriage began to show just after their first wedding anniversary, on 2 June 1953, the day of the Queen's Coronation. 'I had to have new robes made by Victor Stiebel for the Coronation,' Margaret said, 'because the ones I was to have worn were purple which means that they were royal robes and I wasn't allowed to wear them because I wasn't a royal duchess. The last Duchess of Argyll before me was royal. She was The Princess Louise, Duchess of Argyll, who was also Colonel-in-Chief of the combined Argyll and Sutherland Army, but that was a long time ago. There was a very long gap with no duchess. The old Duke had no wife. For sixty or seventy years there was no duchess at all. But the one before me was royal.

'Actually, those robes were worn by the Duchess of Kent on the day of the Coronation, and she was royal.'

Nevertheless, Margaret looked resplendent in her specially made red robes trimmed with ermine. She also wore diamond drop earrings, necklace and bracelet to enhance her striking appearance. She and the Duke arrived at Westminster Abbey early in the morning, equipped with Horlicks tablets to fortify themselves during the long wait for the procession, and were seated with royalty, peers and aristocrats for the start of the ceremony.

But as divorcés, they were not permitted to be received at Court so were not invited to the reception at Buckingham Palace that evening. However, they accepted an invitation to attend a reception given by Madame Massigli, wife of the then French Ambassador, a close friend. As they set off for the grand dinner at the embassy their enthusiasm was dampened by traffic jams and milling sightseers, which forced their chauffeur to make a detour. The Duke, who had had a long tiring day and, doubtless, a glass of Scotch and soda too many, leapt out of the car and stumbled into his club, leaving Margaret to face her hosts alone. She eventually realized that he preferred the environment of his club to her drawing room and went so far as to propose converting the library of her Mayfair home into a replica of White's bar, an offer her husband strenuously rejected. He returned to his favoured haunt whenever he felt like it.

By the spring of 1953, after a year of not-such-wedded-bliss but plenty of hard work in restoring the castle, they were ready to open its doors to the public. The income from tourists, with an estimated 30,000 in the first season, paying their half-crown (twenty-five pence) entry fee, was to contribute to the castle's running costs. The day before the official opening, the Argylls entertained 150 guests at an 'at home'. They included the provosts of county towns, representatives of public bodies, landowners and represent-atives of the tourist agencies and the consular offices. With the pipe band of the 8th Battalion Argyll and Sutherland Highlanders playing from a balcony the guests walked through the drawing room and State Apartments. Among other curiosities, in the dining room they saw the gilt cup and cover given to the eighth Duke in 1875 by Queen Victoria, and a small gold cup given to King George IV at his Coronation. Also on view were famous items such as the Rosewater Dish with medallions of all Queen Victoria's children and the medals struck to celebrate their marriages.

In a speech to the assembled guests, the Duke explained that Inveraray Castle had been the headquarters of Combined Operations Training during the Second World War and it was here that Sir Winston Churchill, the late King George VI and many Chiefs of Staff had held secret meetings.

But there was more on offer for Margaret when the Duke's ex-wife Louise arrived to join in the celebrations. She had sailed in on the *Queen Mary* from a visit to New York accompanied by Colin, their younger son and the Duke's twenty-four-year-old daughter from his first marriage, Jeanne, who had been staying with her grandfather, Lord Beaverbrook, in Montego Bay, Jamaica. Leaving aside her interest in seeing the restoration to the castle, which she had only visited once, Louise wanted to see her elder son, Ian, Marquess of Lorne, who was at school at Glenalmond, Perthshire. No one could have been more displeased at their arrival than Margaret, who, although more than capable of coping in any given situation, took exception to the appearance of her husband's ex-wife and their children, whom she had never met, descending in force so unexpectedly. She felt that they threatened her own future and especially because she was not mother to the heir to the title. The actions of Medea seem as nothing compared to what Margaret had in mind for the visiting triumvirate. She put in motion a devious plot to protect her interests and ensure a stake in the castle in which she had invested so much. This was to involve them in costly legal actions which called into question their credibility – with devastating results.

At the family gathering over dinner Louise announced that next year she intended to remarry. Her bridegroom was to be Robert Claremont Timpson, a forty-five-year-old, six-foot-four-inch-tall, all-American investment banker in New York. She would be his second wife, he her third husband. The Timpson family had come to England from their American home on the Hudson River in 1905 and settled at Preston Candover in Hampshire. All took British nationality with the exception of Robert who, although educated in Britain – at Eton – chose to stay American. She was proud to inform them that her in-laws-to-be had been descended from Chancellor Robert Livingston, who helped to draft the Declaration of Independence and administered the Presidential oath to George Washington in 1789. Although Louise still owned the house at Biarritz and the turreted Château de Lanapoule near Cannes, she would be living in New York. She naturally intended to make frequent trips to Britain to see her sons during their school holidays.

Her news seemed to have no effect on Margaret, who, rather like a nurse, had cultivated an emotional detachment that enabled her to watch those around her either happy or in pain without feeling anything. In time she would illustrate that she could remain unmoved by the malicious hurt she inflicted on others.

Louise wafted away, triumphant in her role as mother of the next Duke of Argyll, secure in her children's future, and full of the happiness that lay ahead of her.

In August, Margaret and the Duke closed the castle doors to the public at the end of the tourist season and set off for Majorca on their annual holiday. In their absence, however, intruders left their mark. During the months in which the castle had been open to the public would-be burglars had ample opportunity to reconnoitre its contents and the lack of security measures. The theft was discovered when a castle gardener on his way to work one morning found the famous Victorian Rosewater Dish and a silver salver lying in the grounds. The gang had used a ladder to reach an unlocked window twenty feet from the ground and had stolen thousands of pounds' worth of gold plate and precious heirlooms including the baton of the Master of the Royal Household in Scotland, covered in plush velvet, studded with small gold thistles and surmounted by a gold lion, a pair of mother-of-pearl lorgnettes with the initial 'N' engraved in mother-of-pearl, said to have been taken from Napoleon's carriage after the battle of Waterloo, a miniature of the seventh Duke of Hamilton, eight small gilt dishes engraved with the Argyll coat of arms, a Victorian silver-gilt bowl and cover and a George II salver, again bearing the Argyll coat of arms.

Six months later Margaret was again the subject of a burglary while entertaining friends at her Mayfair home. It occurred on the eve of a trip she had planned to sail to New York on the *Queen Mary* taking in New Orleans and the Mardi Gras annual festival. The thief climbed up scaffolding at the side of an empty building on the corner of Grosvenor Square and her own street and, with the use of ladders lashed to the side of the scaffolding from about fifteen feet above the ground, crawled along the flat roof of her house. From there he descended to a top-floor window at the back and entered her bedroom where he ransacked her wardrobe and dressing table. Soon after, her maid, Kathleen Carpenter, who had gone up to turn down the bed, found that furs and gems then valued at over six thousand pounds had been stolen. Margaret's faithful butler, Leslie Duckworth, sober for once, summoned the police, but although they arrived almost immediately the stolen items were never found, despite Margaret's having offered a reward. The items were not insured.

When she returned from her American trip she was assailed with more bad news. The Duke explained that he wanted to form his own company to pursue the treasure hunt of the Tobermory sunken galleon and needed further funds to finance the venture. He complained that the castle visitors, with their worthy half-crowns, had hardly contributed to the ruinous running costs and begged his wife for another hundred thousand pounds. Margaret and her father had poured huge amounts of money into the estate since her marriage and although in some ways she was willing to go on doing so, in others she was not. Signs of breakdown were now clearly showing: she accused the Duke of being constantly drunk and neglecting her, and felt that she was now chucking good money after bad. Margaret contributed philanthropically to the running costs of the castle which included food, drink and staff wages amounting to almost four thousand pounds a year, besides which she had to meet the costs of running her London home. The Duke's income of fifteen hundred pounds a year would barely keep the wolf from the door but, although Margaret's private income was considerable, she refused any more help. Her father, too, was disinclined to continue sponsoring his son-in-law, realizing that the marriage was not providing his daughter with the happiness she felt owing to her. She was miserable and even lonely at times and Whigham doubted, as she did, that the marriage could last much longer.

Margaret had always been in charge of her life and the situation in which she found herself was daunting. What she wanted from the marriage was deep, lasting love and romance, but although on her part she had the capacity to provide it, he lacked the ability to reciprocate. When she took a detached look at him, she found that the sandy-haired, solid-looking suave man she had married could be amiable when the mood took him, but he smoked heavily and drank too much. He could seem like Maurice Chevalier with his Gallic charm at one moment and the devil himself the next. She did not find his mercurial nature difficult to cope with but his unpredictability became frustrating when it affected her. If she struck a single discordant note his mood could change immediately. He was a woman's man on the one hand and a man's man on the other, preferring to drink with his male colleagues at his club rather than endure brittle, vacuous conversation in his wife's drawing room. Perhaps because his astrological sign was Gemini (he was born on 19 June 1904), these two separate aspects of his character never came to terms with one another. To Margaret he was becoming tiresome and boring; he was eleven years older than her but she needed the vitality of a man eleven years younger, and their preferences for different lifestyles drove them further and further apart. Not for her the discomfort of country life, wearing head-scarves, woollies and brogues, attending fêtes and going to church on Sundays, mingling with the local community, but life in the fast lane in London. The sedate stately rooms of Inveraray Castle threatened to throttle her fun-loving, gregarious nature.

The Duke's own responsibilities lay in the administration of the castle and running the vast Argyll estates. He craved the quiet and restfulness of Scotland after incarceration in a prisoner-of-war camp, and, equipped with a pair of binoculars, he enjoyed bird-watching, or indulged his love of gardening.

Margaret was aware of his infidelities, but he had been careful enough to leave no tangible evidence. Had Margaret proof of his escapades she would have used it. The break-up of the marriage, however, could be blamed on them both. There was no sense of companionship between them: sex had been the element that bound them together and when that went, so did love. Also, they had lost respect for each other. He could be as dogmatic and selfish as her, and in the male-dominated society of that era, he had the upper hand. If she showed signs of insecurity it was because she was frightened that he would divorce her. She knew that she could not divorce him without his consent, neither did she wish to do so, and besides she was still, in name at least, a Catholic. Her son and her daughter were devout in their faith and she had them to consider.

'He had great personal charm which he used to influence people all his life,' Margaret said. 'He also toyed with me as a cat plays with a mouse, and every time he sensed that I had come to the end of my tether, he would then choose to become his most agreeable self, ready to do anything to please me. He was such an attractive man and I was a mere pawn in his hands. Even my father, who was such a clever man, was putty in his hands.'

Soon afterwards Margaret, too, began to find her satisfaction and companionship elsewhere – far away from Scotland, the Duke and the confines of the castle gates. She found them on her own doorstep in Mayfair. Her associations with amusing, handsome men, who could flatter, escort and dance with her, grew from her longing for the swirling London life of which she had been deprived in Scotland.

The Duke was all too aware that she needed escorts to take her to film premières and parties and to entertain her at her favourite nightclubs and, since he had chosen for himself the seclusion of Scotland and Inveraray Castle, went along with her whims. His high tolerance level stemmed from his five years in the POW camp and he was unable to adjust to her gregarious lifestyle which was so alien to him.

She had a flair for self-publicity and attracted press photographers as a lighted lamp attracts moths. But the Duke was not pleased to read reports of her social rounds in the glossy magazines: she carried the Argyll name, after all, and might bring it into disrepute. He protested vehemently in the autumn of 1954, three years after their marriage, when he heard that she had installed a young admirer in the mews cottage in the grounds of her Upper Grosvenor Street home. After he learnt that her lover had been there for over six weeks, the Duke rebuked her on the telephone from Inveraray Castle. 'But surely I'm allowed to have – to have friends,' she stammered back. 'How can you escort me yourself when you're stuck up at that dreary hole in Scotland for most of the time?'

With the deterioration of their relationship the Duke became reconciled to the situation and cared less and less about the amount of time he spent in London. However, he drew the line when Margaret began to invite her guests to Inveraray Castle. But she was undeterred by his protests and went so far as to invite a man who was eventually named as one of her adulterous lovers by the Duke when he filed his divorce petition.

At this time, Margaret was often seen at social functions and dining with the handsome Baron Sigismund von

Braun, a diplomat at the German Embassy. His brother, the famous rocket scientist Dr Wernher von Braun, had invented the deadly V-2s that perpetrated so much destruction in London during the war. The Duke had every reason to detest the man, with his prisoner-of-war record, even though von Braun was in fact anti-Nazi, yet Margaret invited him and his wife to spend a holiday with them at Inveraray Castle. The Duke dreaded the day of their arrival, but matters grew worse when Margaret and the charming Baron went for long walks together in the castle grounds. To add insult to injury, he had to conduct polite conversation with the Baroness while they strolled beside his carefully tended borders. At first, the Duke felt that Margaret was impressed with the German because he flattered her and fed her considerable ego, and also because his position at the embassy carried with it a certain cachet that Margaret found appealing – but he realized later that the Baron had become her steady lover. He remembered Sarah Bernhardt's epithet: 'Egotism in an imbecile is a vice. In an intelligent spirit it is a virtue.' He doubted that his wandering wife belonged to the latter category.

A member of Margaret's set, and one who remained a lifelong friend, was the beautiful British comedy actress Moira Lister. The star of stage and screen, the witty, glamorous blonde married the French Vicomte d'Orthez whose family were noted for their wine produced in south-west

France, near Lourdes. Moira remembers von Braun: 'Sigismund von Braun was a great lad about town at that time,' she recalled. 'He was a man of enormous charm and a real ladies' man. He was about five foot eleven tall and very good-looking. You know, when the Germans put on the charm you can't resist it. I dined with him and I danced with him. He was in great demand at the time.'

There is no doubt that he satisfied Margaret's demand.

Margaret and the Duke accepted the inevitable. They knew that they were no longer compatible, but he bided his time, giving her enough rope in the knowledge that eventually she would hang herself with it.

CHAPTER FIVE

Trouble Ahead

A T Frances Sweeny's coming-out in 1955 no one could
have been more conscious of the changing times
than her mother. Margaret compared her own presentation to Queen Mary in 1930 amid the grandeur, formality
and elegance of British royal tradition with the informal
garden-party atmosphere of Buckingham Palace presided
over by Queen Elizabeth II, who received the débutantes
and their mothers dressed in afternoon frocks. Gone were
the days of court dresses, diamonds and pearls, trains and
large feather fans, with the Prince Aly Khans and other
foreign royalty in attendance.

Upper-middle-class young ladies now earned their own
living, many becoming models, referred to as mannequins

in an earlier age, and with their haughty look, cultured backgrounds and elegant turn-out, began marrying into the peerage. They were accepted by society.

The young Frances, half-American and a devout Catholic, had had a perfect upbringing, educated in England and finished in Florence and Paris, and on a dreary winter day in early March, Margaret accompanied her daughter to Buckingham Palace looking, for once, far from one of the 'best-dressed women in Britain'. She was criticized for wearing clothes and a hat seen on public occasions four years before – perhaps because she did not wish to upstage her daughter on such a big day, but in fact, she had worn black because her mother had died four days earlier and she was in mourning.

Amid the publicity that Margaret had always attracted, Frances arrived in the fashionable Dior-length day dress, corn-coloured, designed by her mother's favourite couturier, Norman Hartnell, a fur stole round her shoulders to shield her from the biting cold. Although Frances was much photographed and reported in the press she stood little chance of competing with her mother's celebrated beauty, even though, cast much in the same mould, she was also beautiful, charming, well mannered and much liked. She, too, became 'débutante of the year'.

In complete contrast to Margaret's own presentation, held in Mayfair twenty-five years before, when afterwards four hundred guests, attired in white-tie and ballgowns, bedecked in enough diamonds to strip a Kimberley mine, had danced the night away to Ambrose and his band, Frances's coming-out party was held at Claridge's with a hundred people for dinner wearing black-tie and another seven hundred at the dance which followed. A most important guest, made conspicuous by his absence, was Frances's stepfather, the Duke, who was said officially to be deeply engrossed in the waters of Tobermory Bay in another attempt to find the elusive sunken vessel. Margaret had organized the décor of the ballroom with an all-pink theme, an idea pinched from Stephen Tennant who had held an 'all pink party', with all pink food – prawns and salmon were followed by strawberries and pink cream – pink table-cloths, napkins and pink flower decorations, while pink-tinted doves cooed contentedly from above. Margaret drew the line at the latter. Dressed for the ball, again by her mother's favourite designer, Hartnell, Frances was applauded by all in the reels, which were led by the piper from Inveraray Castle. In sharp contrast to the Scottish flavour laid on with a trowel, the cabaret act consisted of the then hit group, the Deep River Boys, more her mother's taste than Frances's.

That summer, the time came for a family holiday. Margaret, the Duke, Frances and Brian had been invited to a two-week bash by the famed professional party-giver

Elsa Maxwell, on behalf of the multi-millionaire Greek shipping tycoon Stavros Niarchos on his six-thousand-ton yacht, the *Archilleus*. He had been asked by Queen Frederika of Greece to arrange a VIP cruise to show off the beauty of the Greek islands, then a rare sight for visitors. The guest list included the two hundred most eligible people in the world.

'When I read the invitation I expected Ian's usual anti-social reaction,' Margaret said, 'but to my amazement he jumped at the idea. The trip, sailing from Venice, was one Ian jumped at the chance of making and he exclaimed on receiving the invitation, "I don't care who else is going. I'll be there with bells on." About a week before we were due to join Elsa and the ship in Venice Ian announced that he was not going after all,' she continued, 'and I was left the painful task of making excuses for him to Elsa.' The trio spent the first week in Venice where they joined in the festivities together with John D. Rockefeller Jnr, Randolph Hearst, Mrs Perle Mesta, Olivia de Havilland and one of the Chrysler heiresses, Mrs Byron Foy, after which they boarded the yacht and set out on a sea of champagne. The first port of call was Capri, followed by the Greek islands during which time Margaret renewed acquaintance on board ship with Loelia, Duchess of Westminster, and the man she had wanted to marry when she was seventeen, Prince Aly Khan.

On their return to England, Margaret was pleased to accept another invitation, this time to the Paris wedding of Barbara Hutton, who had chosen Baron von Cramm as her sixth husband. The two remained friends through the years, even when Barbara's mind began to wander and she refused to walk on the pavement, instead being carried everywhere by her burly chauffeur.

To round off the season of travelling and partying in her efforts to launch Frances into society, Margaret took her daughter on her first visit to New York, flying from London Airport in time for Christmas. Once there, she despatched Frances to friends in Palm Beach for a fortnight while she returned home to London.

Back in Britain, she discovered, to her relief, that the Duke, almost at his wits' end to find the money to keep Inveraray Castle afloat, had been left a large sum by a complete stranger, an eccentric but highly intelligent eighty-eight-year-old woman he had never met. It arrived like manna from heaven. Mrs Eliza Sale, from Hove in Sussex, claimed that she was a distant relative of his family, the only daughter of one Joseph McGregor Campbell, a wealthy London jeweller. The likelihood of any connection with the Duke's family may only have lain in Mrs Sale's having been a member of the Clan Campbell of which the Duke was chief. She had left £140,000 altogether, after duty, and after a few other bequests, including £1,000 and a dog to her companion for twenty-one years, a Miss Elizabeth Hicks, the Duke would eventually receive investments worth about £35,000 after the expiry of the life interest of two beneficiaries. The Duke, at last, had means independent of his wife.

As a further boost to his income the Duke lent his name to a brand of men's socks for distribution in America. Known as 'Authentic Argylls' they were promoted in the journal *Men's Wear* in a full-page advertisement in which the Duke held a pair of scarlet and chocolate tartan socks, with a label showing his coat of arms – a boar's head, two lions supporting a shield, and the family motto, *Forget not*.

During the hectic London season of 1956, Margaret was again escorted by a series of handsome men and the Duke remained in Scotland. The coast was decidedly clear, and she made the most of it.

Margaret joined him at Inveraray Castle that October, and while she was there, she received the shock of her life. It had nothing to do with the Duke, but engendered in her so much hate and possessiveness that she forgot her own recent indiscretions in New York and London.

Unknown to her, on one of his crossings from New York to Southampton in 1947 her father had met a charming divorcée, Mrs Jane Brooke, who was thirty-five years younger than he was and a year younger than Margaret. She had a daughter by her first marriage. George Whigham, whose wife was confined to a wheelchair for the last fifteen years of her life, invited Jane to dine with him and his wife at their Dorchester flat. Their friendship continued platonically over the next eight years. After Mrs Whigham died in 1955 they began to spend more time together, until on 31 October 1956 they decided to marry – and did so at Caxton Hall that morning. Margaret's father telephoned her shortly after the ceremony to tell her his news. Instead of congratulating him she was numbed at first and then shocked. She had met Jane Brooke once, briefly, with her parents and nothing had prepared her for her father's marrying the attractive auburn-haired woman so suddenly and without telling her. 'How could you do this to me, Daddy?' she reproached him and, after the news had sunk in, she burst into tears. Fearful of sharing her father and of losing her inheritance and now needing his support more than ever, as she approached the first of the seven High Court actions that followed each other in rapid succession, she was fired with resentment against her new stepmother.

Her father's new-found happiness in contrast with the shaky state of her marriage caused Margaret to sink into devastating depths of despair. She needed more than ever the exclusive single-minded dedication of the old man who had always stood by her and who had, by his power and wealth, always kissed it better. She also missed his guidance. The lack of a restraining influence led to a series of ill-fated court cases.

CHAPTER SIX

Dark December

NINETEEN fifty-seven saw the end of George Whigham's chairmanship of Celanese. He was nearly seventy and had seen too many takeovers and mergers. British Celanese finally amalgamated with its rival Courtauld. Margaret's father, now remarried, had settled down with her stepmother at Cookham Dean, Berkshire, and Margaret was still painfully jealous.

Her son Brian won a scholarship to Oxford at the age of seventeen and Frances was thinking seriously of taking a husband by the time she reached twenty. She had been courted by a charming young man of Egyptian extraction but her mother had other ideas for her. The Duke of Rutland, who had succeeded to the title aged twenty-one, had been married to Anne Cumming Bell, but was now divorced. He had one daughter by her.

At the end of that same year, 1957, Margaret had realized that she might stand a chance of marrying off her daughter to the eligible rich Duke whose estates included Belvoir Castle, and the magnificent sixteenth-century Haddon Hall in Derbyshire. But she needed to act fast. There was stiff competition from other eager mothers. Although the Duke was eighteen years older than twenty-one-year-old Frances, he was handsome, charming and distinguished-looking with a pleasant manner, and was a decided 'catch' who had already dated Frances several times. Margaret decided quickly to arrange a winter holiday in the Middle East, leaving for Beirut on 29 January 1958, with plans to visit Jordan, Iraq, Iran and Israel. She got tickets for her and the Duke, and for Frances and the Duke of Rutland, but because of the acrimony in their marriage Ian Argyll refused to go, giving Margaret ten days to cancel his bookings. Margaret, with cast-iron determination to seal the match, set off on holiday with Frances and Rutland. It was a new role for her to play gooseberry.

She had the foresight to inform the press of their journey in advance, and wherever they went photographers and journalists reported their every move. The ploy worked. The courtship blossomed and Charles Rutland proposed to Frances in the romantic atmosphere of the Accadia

Hotel in Tel Aviv. She accepted. Fleet Street, as well, were ecstatic and their engagement was announced in *The Times*. However, one hurdle – and an important one at that – had to be overcome. Frances was Catholic, her fiancé Protestant. Also as he was divorced they could not marry in either a Catholic or an Anglican church. They were married on 15 May 1958 in a civil ceremony at Caxton Hall. The reception afterwards was held at Claridge's, complete with the piper, Ronnie McCallum, from Inveraray Castle and guests that included the Dowager Duchess of Rutland, Frances's father Charles Sweeny and the Duke of Argyll. Dressed, as usual, by Norman Hartnell, Frances wore a pink organza dress, its skirt lined with pink ostrich features which peeped out from below the hem, with a close-fitting pink ostrich feather hat.

The couple set off on honeymoon for a secret destination. Mother and daughter were blissfully happy, Frances because she had married the man she loved and Margaret because her ambition for her daughter had been realized. However, Margaret knew that her own marriage was on the rocks and was filled with trepidation for her future even if her daughter's seemed secure. She had to keep face at least in public, even if the Duke had it in for her while he watched her in action.

He allowed her to resume her role as mistress of Inveraray Castle – for the time being.

The Inveraray Games had been held annually in the castle grounds until the event had lapsed during Neil Duke's time and Margaret revived it as her main task in that year. Two of the neighbouring towns, Lochgilphead and Campbeltown, had famous Gaelic choirs and Margaret induced them to sing for the townspeople who joined in the chorus. It was her last public duty.

The Duke had been invited to visit the Argyll and Sutherland Highlanders in Cyprus by their colonel to boost morale. He was determined to go without Margaret. But nothing could have persuaded her to stay at home. Her role as Duchess of Argyll was still undisputed from the outside and she had no intention of giving up the illusion of glamour. There was no love left between them and, although the Duke resented her intrusion, there seemed no stopping her.

The Cyprus trip proved a curtain-raiser to the disastrous tour of Canada the Duke made soon after. He visited the Canadian Argyll and Sutherland Highlanders in Toronto two months later, with Margaret once again insisting on joining him. They set sail on the *Homeric*. On the voyage Margaret became smitten by a handsome young man of half her age, accompanied by his parents, and intent on seeking a business appointment in Canada. The Duke ignored her flirtation, and on his trips to Toronto and Montreal gave no further thought to it.

He decided to fly on to Boston and New York from Canada, before returning to London to fulfil an engagement in London, expecting his wife to accompany him. But she had other ideas. The young man was in tow in New York and she decided to remain there. 'You're just a stupid, jealous old man,' she smirked when he reproached her, and announced that she would see him in London at Christmastime.

The Duke returned alone, and when Margaret joined him in London a week before Christmas, he became convinced that their marriage had no hope of survival. He tried to reason with her, blaming the break-up of their relationship on her associations with other men, but she dismissed this, explaining that she was still young enough to enjoy herself. She told him that she had made plans to spend the New Year without him at the house of some friends in Henley-on-Thames. He did not realize then that one of her boyfriends would be among the guests.

The New Year saw the Duke begin his search for evidence that would give him grounds to divorce her, while she, attempting desperately to divert his action, set about discrediting the people he loved or with whom he had any dealings: his secretary, some of their mutual friends, his children and then, finally, himself, when she counter-petitioned for divorce naming her stepmother as co-respondent. The latter was a futile attempt to curtail his own action, naming several men. This time the Duke was determined he would not allow himself to be divorced. Neither would he refund any of the money that had been advanced to him.

The battle began in earnest with the Duke's next tour, this time of the Campbell communities in Australia and New Zealand, which he had determined to undertake alone. Margaret, however, bought her own ticket and insisted on accompanying him. It was during this trip Down Under that he secured the graphic evidence of her infidelities.

In Sydney, while he was dressing for an engagement, he went into Margaret's bedroom to borrow a comb and noticed her red leather engagement diary lying open on her dressing table. At first he hardly glanced at it but then something compelled him to take a closer look. Interspersed between details of trains caught and cheques cashed, she had jotted down notes recording the dates, times and names of appointments with half a dozen different men. He flicked through the pages and quickly deduced that she had had affairs with one or two, and certainly with Baron Sigismund von Braun, the German diplomat. The Duke already knew she had been enjoying a love-affair with von Braun, but, until now, had no written proof. She had kept unusual diaries: each covered a four-year period so that she could compare what she had done on the same day and at the same time in preceding years: each page was divided into four, giving the same day of the month for four consecutive years. The one that the Duke seized, with a mixture of anger and triumph, covered the years from 1956 to 1959.

As he flicked through the pages, she entered the room. 'What are you doing with my property? Give it to me,' she demanded. She rushed at him and snatched it from him. It was too late, he told her calmly, he had seen everything. When he accused her of adultery she made no attempt to deny it.

'What was I supposed to do with you stuck – stuck up at that damned castle all the time?' she stammered, her diction now impaired by fright. 'You've hardly taken me out for years. All you think about is poking about in your bloody garden. You don't like parties, and you hate nightclubs. You loathe to entertain. What was I supposed to do?'

He tried to reason with her, to remind her that their agreement had been that in exchange for his spending time with her in London she was to spend a reasonable amount of time with him at Inveraray Castle.

'You and your old castle,' she spat back. 'I couldn't live there and I've told you so.' It was Scarlett O'Hara and Joan Crawford rolled into one. 'You won't live in London. What am I supposed to do on my own? Can you wonder that I go out with other men?'

There was no more to say. He packed the next day and left for London, abandoning her in the hotel suite. She had to make her own arrangements for the journey home.

'That trip to Australia was an absolutely wonderful trip. Really royal, and the last time we were together as man and wife. It was the end of the marriage. It was really the most fabulous trip, and I thought at last Ian's beginning to make sense. Beginning to stop drinking. Beginning to take himself and his job seriously. And I was pretty happy about him, and then *bang*.'

Incensed by the knowledge of Margaret's infidelities, the Duke needed further written proof of her adultery to secure a divorce, particularly since he had been unable to hold on to the engagement book. But he knew that he would find more information in her earlier diaries and in possible letters she might have received from her lovers, and that she kept them locked away in her house in London.

The Duke seized the opportunity to gain access to them on his return to London ahead of her on 20 April, when he began a systematic search. He knew that she would not be back for at least a fortnight since she had planned to visit friends in New York *en route* from Sydney. 'Her diaries were in an open drawer in her desk,' the Duke said, 'and some private letters were in a locked cabinet where I knew she kept them. I had a key made for the cabinet by a locksmith and had it opened. I took the diaries from the open drawer in her desk and several letters, many of which I had written to her.'

At the back of the bookcase in Margaret's study he came across several large bundles of letters, and two of her earlier four-year diaries for the periods 1948 to 1951, and 1952 to 1955. He turned his attention to a manilla envelope addressed to the Duchess of Argyll. It contained two sets of notes, evidently sent with Christmas or birthday presents, and a sheet of white paper folded round some photographs. 'In two prints Margaret appeared naked with a naked man,' the Duke revealed. 'There were other pictures of a naked man, showing only part of his body. These were captioned.' They became known as the pornographic photographs of the 'headless man', and had been taken on an early Polaroid instamatic camera. But the document that shocked him most was a sheet of a Paris hotel's headed writing paper with fragments of words cut out from harmless letters written by his ex-wife, Louise, mother of his sons, together with her signature. They were pasted on to the sheet of writing paper questioning the paternity of his two children. Several more blank sheets of the hotel writing paper confirmed his suspicion that Margaret had compiled the document. It was on the strength of this evidence that he determined finally to separate himself from her for ever.

He took the diaries, letters and forged papers to his bank where he lodged them in a safety box until handing them over to his solicitors whom he instructed to begin divorce proceedings. However, he needed one other item as evidence to support his case, Margaret's current four-year diary for the years 1956 to 1959, which he had skimmed through in Australia, but since she kept this with her at all times he had to wait for an opportunity to seize it.

Margaret returned to London in May, in time to celebrate the birth of her daughter's first baby, on 8 May, a son and heir to the Rutland dukedom. Born at Westminster Hospital the little Marquess of Granby was named David but controversy arose over whether he should be baptized as an Anglican or a Catholic. Both parents were devout members of their own Church. Considerable acrimony ensued between the two families but it was finally agreed that David would be Catholic. It was said at the time that a priest had had to be virtually smuggled into Belvoir Castle to conduct the service.

When she got home, Margaret was shocked not only at the disappearance of private papers, letters and the other items from her desk and cupboard but also because the Duke had packed his personal belongings and left her. He had moved to nearby Claridge's Hotel.

'He didn't leave a single thing behind. Not a handkerchief or a tie-pin. Then I looked through the desk and found that he had taken my letters. He raided this house. And he did that with his second wife, Louise, too. He took all his letters from him to her. And in a way, I had kept his letters to me because there were very happy times in that marriage. It wasn't bad by all means. He took all his letters to me.'

But letters of a different nature were the subject of the train of events that led from one court action to another, many of which overlapped. Margaret had visited Paris to see the new spring collections, and arranged to see the Duke on her return. She produced from her handbag a sheet of her Paris hotel's headed writing paper which she handed to him. She told him that she had copied out extracts from letters she had come across in Paris.

He read the missive which contained passages from various letters supposedly written by his ex-wife, Louise, to another friend, containing highly damaging statements about his family and himself. Margaret told the story that she had been to see the friend in Paris who showed her the letters. She had realized at once the gravity of the allegations contained in them, and asked to read them alone. Left on her own, she explained, she had copied on to the sheet of paper that the Duke now held the salient points of the letters.

She produced from her handbag an anonymous letter she said she herself had received that morning, and showed it to him. It was written in the same hand and on the same Paris hotel writing paper. It exclaimed boldly, 'HOPING

THAT THIS WILL HELP A VERY GOOD WOMAN TO
REVEAL THE LIES OF A VERY EVIL ONE.' A few
days later, Margaret said she received another poison-pen
letter, delivered by hand to her house in Upper Grosvenor
Street. It began with the following sentence, 'I AM OLD
AND OF POOR HEALTH, BUT I DO NOT LIKE TO
SEE ANYONE LIVING A LIE.' Frances also received one
of these anonymous letters and took it to her mother,
who showed it to the Duke. The writer of the poison-pen
letter continued that he or she had 'written evidence'
to support the malicious allegations referred to, 'facts'
that were designed to bring distress and disrepute to the
Duke's name and family, alleging that he was not the
father of his and Louise's two sons and therefore that
they were not entitled to inherit the dukedom of Argyll
or the estates.

These destructive lies also became the subject of gossip
which began to circulate in London. The Duke turned to
Scotland Yard for help.

Margaret, however, had not realized that the Duke had
found the blueprints for these letters when he raided the
house and that he had put into action his plan to expose
her as the author of them. He had contacted Louise, who
lived in New York, telling her about the letters, that they
were forgeries and that he was convinced that their author
was none other than his current wife. She, he said, had had

them delivered to herself and her daughter anonymously. Louise set off straight away for London to sue Margaret and to stop her from doing further harm to her and the children.

'Ian told me certain things about his two children,' Margaret confided, 'that I didn't know about. The two sons by his previous marriage to Louise. How could I have known about it? I wasn't around when he was married to Louise. It wasn't a happy marriage, and during the marriage he was picking up girls for five years.

'Ian told me and my father certain things about those two boys which we obviously didn't know about before we came on the scene. And Ian believed what he told us, and he told the trustees this too. Well, she, the mother of these boys, and one of their trustees as well, was so furious, that she started to begin a legal action against Ian. She came over to England and saw Ian's secretary, Yvonne MacPherson. They knew each other and apparently Louise told Yvonne, "I'm going to bring a case against Ian Argyll for what he is saying about *our* children." And the secretary, who loathed me, and I don't know why, because all I'd done was to be bloody kind to her, said to Louise, "Don't attack Ian. Attack Margaret instead." Ian came to see me. He was terribly upset. Terribly worried. Sweat was really pouring down his face. He said to me, "You're to be sued by..."' She stammered, 'You know, her actual name was Louise – O-U-I, as in Louise, and she used to call herself Oui-Oui, the French for 'yes', and spelt it that way, but I spelt it Wee-Wee and put it that way in all the legal documents, but they scratched it out! I said, "Well, let her. Let her go ahead and sue away. What can she do to me?" Up to this time I had never had any law case in public. The MacPherson case was pending, hanging over my head, though, waiting to come to court. So I said, "Good God, how much more of this am I going to have?" And Ian said, "She's going to sue you, and the case must *never* come to court." So I said, "Well, don't worry Ian, it won't. I don't know what it's all about, but it *won't*. There's no reason why it should. I don't know what the hell she thinks, she must be out of her *mind*."

'Well, along it came. Along came the long brown envelope. Actually, I remember when it came. It came the day my daughter Frances had her first boy, David, and I was very anxious that Ian should come up to the hospital with me, all the time she was having it. Because it was a tremendous thrill; my first grandchild. And, knowing Ian, I thought that if he ever sees this thing, the writ related to the poison-pen letters, he won't come. So I didn't let him see it, and I pushed it into my bag. But on our way to the hospital he said, "I know you've got a writ in that bag."

'I said, "OK, Ian, it's there. But it doesn't mean anything. Let's get to the hospital now and concentrate on Frances.

We'll talk about this later." And he *was* there at the time my first grandchild was born. I mean, I was struggling for things which should be normal. And after we got back from the hospital, he was grey with fright. *Grey*. And I said, "Ian, don't *worry*. First of all, it's ridiculous to say that I said this, because I wasn't there at the time. How could I have said it? You know perfectly well after all these years that I wouldn't say this. We'll sort it out. Don't fuss. It will be OK."

'When the case came up, Magda Buchel, one of my best friends, who was going to give evidence against me in the MacPherson case too and Diana Napier, who had also joined in the gang, both got into court and said they'd heard me saying this about the children's paternity. It's a *dreadful* thing to say against children.'

The main reason for Margaret's attempts to discredit the boys' paternity lay in the fact that Margaret wanted nothing more than to have a son of her own who would become heir to the Duke of Argyll, benefit from all the money she had invested in Inveraray and secure her future as dowager. Then she would have it all: a duchess herself, having a daughter who was also a duchess, a son who would be a duke, and also grandsons who would be dukes in the future.

In order to fulfil her bizarre scheme, having failed to become pregnant she decided to plan a fake pregnancy, in an effort to have her stepsons disinherited and replace them with her own child. Thus, Margaret summoned her long-standing friend Diana Napier to luncheon and said to her, 'Darling, I want you to go to Venice at my expense. I would like you to use your Polish contacts to adopt a newborn child or get a newborn child over from Poland to Venice.' Pressed by Diana for an explanation, Margaret said, 'I have padded my tummy with a cushion and put it about that I am pregnant. I want to fake a pregnancy and go to Venice and bring back the Polish child as the Duke's son.' She went on to explain that she had put word abroad that the Duke's rightful heirs were illegitimate and once she had succeeded in removing them from the direct line, her own 'son' would succeed to the title and the estate.

Diana Napier, a worldly woman, laughed in shocked disbelief. She dismissed Margaret's request with, 'Don't be stupid, dear,' and said that she would not become involved in such a farcical scheme, explaining to Margaret that she would be 'mad' to say anything disparaging about the Duke and his former wife's children.

'Well, it would have been a hideous case, don't you see?' Margaret said many years later, pleading innocence to the charges. 'With all these friends making me the fiend, trying to take away these boys' parentage? And they would have got up and said I had broadcast it. That I had said it over and over again in front of people, and they went into the box on *oath* to say that I had said all this about those boys.

'The other two people who gave evidence against me were my secretary, Mrs MacPherson, and the other, a terribly close friend.'

Margaret was frightened: she had had no idea of the significance of the slander she had spread. It hadn't occurred to her that she would end up in court, possibly in prison. She had deluded herself that her few close friends would perjure themselves to save her skin. She felt the whole affair would be 'ugly' if it got to court and she was made to look bad. With almost no experience of the law, she believed that the issue was a sort of game and that it would all come right in the end. If she got hurt, Daddy would kiss it better.

Margaret was very conscious of her position as a duchess and, equipped as she was with money, social standing, beauty and grace, it was unthinkable to her that anyone would question her integrity. It was as though she had set herself beyond the law. It seemed she felt herself to be royal – never to be doubted, questioned or crossed.

Because of what she had said, the Duke's, his ex-wife's and their children's futures were at stake but she failed to understand the ramifications.

She did, however, add: 'Ian was worried stiff about this case ever coming off. Worried *stiff*, but things were getting out of hand by now. He had written a letter to the trustees saying, "I don't want my son to have such and such, *because* such and such." And that's when *she*, Louise Timpson, his ex-wife, blew up and said, "Now it's on paper, I'm going to go to town on him." But she went to town on me instead. It was a nightmare. So I said to Ian, "Don't fuss. I promise you it won't come to court. I don't want to go to court. Nobody does." And he replied, "Well, I'm leaving you until you've settled it." And that's when he packed up every bloody thing and left me. He knew I adored him. Knew I was an idiot. And he thought, "The only way that I've got is to walk out of her life, and she'll be so miserable." And that's exactly what happened. I was in despair. And my heart was broken.'

The Duke had several solid reasons for leaving her once and for all. He was wholly convinced of her adulteries. She had openly called his sons bastards. She had libelled and slandered his secretary. The latter court case was pending. He had every reason to go. Margaret takes up the story: 'He told me that Louise wanted me to go under an injunction. To sign an injunction to say that I would never mention this again. Of course, the word "again" means that you have mentioned it before. I didn't realize this at the time. I didn't realize that an injunction is a classic admission of guilt. If you are under an injunction you are classically saying you have done something. So I said, "I'll go under any old injunction. I don't want to talk about your two bloody children anyway. What the hell does it matter?"

'And he said that if I signed it, he would come back to me. Then little Ian, the young Lord Lorne [the Duke's son and heir who inherited the dukedom on the death of his father in 1973] got on the telephone and I said, "Ian, if I *am* perfectly prepared to sign this thing to your mother which completes your happiness, how do I know that it won't be shown all over town?"

'He replied, "It's a very nasty thing to sign, I'm sure. And I don't know what it's all about, but listen, Margaret, you know me. I'm a gentleman, and my father's a gentleman. We wouldn't dream of showing this injunction around."

'All I can say is that they were terrified. *Terrified.* It would *always* cast a doubt, you see.

'I think what Ian originally said was true. I don't think it's true of the other, but I think it's only the second one.' She was referring to his sons and implying that the Duke had told her that the first son was legitimate and the second one was not. 'And I didn't have a son. I didn't have a child by Ian. It wasn't going to alter *my* life.'

The crux of the matter was that she did not have a son by the Duke. Although she said that it would not have altered her life, she knew that if she had produced one, and he had become heir to the Duke, she would have been secure in her marriage. Margaret knew that the Duke intended to divorce her and that this was the only hold she could have over him and the Argyll dynasty.

But to have imagined that she was clever enough to succeed in her plan…

She made clear what her intentions had been when she added: 'If I'd had a son by Ian, it would have made more sense, you see. So then Lord Lorne, young Ian, said in this smooth voice of his, "You know perfectly well, Margaret, it will just be between us. If you will just sign, it will make Mummy happy, and then even my father and me will be together again." I mean, silk couldn't have been as smooth as his voice on the telephone was. And I was absolutely distraught. If anybody was ever out of their mind, I was. And I went to the lawyers. My husband was terribly persuasive as all crooks are, and he said to me, "Look. I'll take you away on a trip if you just sign this, and finish this thing." The brain-washing! It was just like that film *Gaslight*.

'So I went to my lawyers and told them that I would sign the injunction. But they told me that it would be terribly dangerous to do so because if I were under an injunction I would have admitted that I had slandered these two children. And then I said, "I don't care. I don't care. I want my husband back. Bring me the papers in triplicate and let me sign them." I had had very bad lawyers in the past. I wouldn't listen to lawyers. But this time they were right. I can smell a lawyer. I know all the legal terms now, but until then I didn't understand them at all. I thought they were God. Now I realize they're anything but God. They take their instructions from you, and if you're tough with them, they work much harder for you.

I just used to say, "What do I do? What do I do?" Now I say, "We're going to do this, this and this." And they're *not* God.

'Anyway, they said they were horrified and that I was out of my mind. But my only concern was to get my husband back. And I don't think he meant it. I don't think he knew what he wanted, then. I know he was terrified of the case. He came back to me afterwards, for a night or two at the Ritz Hotel in Paris. Then he left me again. It was torture. It was agony. It was a terrible summer. It was actually the summer the legal papers came, and I never went through such a ghastly summer in my life. So I signed this damned injunction, and my husband had it heard up at Oxford so that the press wouldn't get hold of it, in order to protect the children. But I had the sense to take out the word "again". I told the lawyers that I will say that I will never mention it, because I don't want to. But I certainly would not sign anything that said, "again", because that would mean that I had said it in the first place, and I never bloody well had. I had to think of that, not of the lawyers. So we had it all heard up at Oxford with the greatest of silence. No press. And I made the grave mistake of going down to the South of France to stay with some tremendously social people afterwards, called Heinz, of the Heinz 57 varieties. I went to try to cheer myself up. I was very miserable. It was a great mistake. When you're unhappy you should never do it in a social place, because the whole damn world sees you're unhappy. I was in floods of tears half the time. It was a great mistake.

'*Who* should follow hot on my heels to stay with another hostess, equally well known, but Ian and his daughter from his first marriage, Jeanne, with the injunction that I had signed in their hands, spraying it round every dinner party. There were two headlines in the newspapers which I did not put in my scrapbooks, because I've got to think of my grandchildren too. There was a great huge article given by Louise Timpson saying that she had made me sign the injunction, and that she got seven thousand pounds of the money I had to pay. All of which we did our best to keep quiet for the children's sake at the Oxford hearing, and she blasts it. She doesn't say what it's about. She says she's made me go under an injunction, and she's handing this out all over the place.

'Ian and his son got hold of a man called Peter Baker on the *Express* newspaper. Peter Baker ran the [William] Hickey column. He told me that Ian had called him up to say, "Come round and have a drink at St James's with me and my son." So he did, and Ian told him, "Print this. This is the injunction." So Peter said to him, "(a) I can't. And (b) I don't want to." He knew it was bloody dangerous. And Peter Baker came up to me to say, "Look what you're up against." It was a nightmare with those two.

'Then, to show how careful I had to be, a great friend of ours called Bill Thornton contacted me. He was an air-marshal and a perfect darling. He was an alcoholic. He's now dead. He was also a great friend of Ian's and he had a great influence on him. When I was in trouble, I used to get Bill to help me. And he said, "Look, I'm going to have one try at getting the two of you together." This was after the injunction. I had already signed it, and paid over the money [£10,000 with costs]. "I think if you two met, you could come to an understanding and get the bloody divorce out of the way," he said. I had already offered Ian a divorce. I had said, "You can have an affair with an unnamed woman, but don't attack me!" So, I must say, *I* muffed it.

'He got Ian around here. He came in, a huge cigarette holder, looking pompous as all hell, but I blew my top when he said, "I have the divorce petition being sent around by my legal advisers to the Quarter Sessions in Edinburgh, naming two men." I think at this point it was only two men. He'd only got two men. And I cut him short. I said, "Take your petition and do what you want with it. You and your *damned* gang! Your daughter, that bloody secretary—" I lost my temper, and I blew the chance to get him back. It was my fault. I really lost my head and lost my temper. It was his attitude and his manner when he came in, and I knew Ian by this time, and I blew it. I just blew it. I blew the chance.'

True to her contradictory nature, Margaret had become confused by her own emotions. She said on the one hand that she blew her chance to get him back, implying that she didn't really want to lose him, and on the other hand she told him to get out of her life.

The Duke had been the pawn of the three rich, beautiful brides who had kept him, and his estate, afloat. Even now Margaret, not convinced that she had lost him for good, believed she could buy him back. She felt that by paying him a sum of money and admitting to him that she had had at least one lover, he would take her back – and she would not lose her status as Duchess nor expose herself to a messy divorce. He had seen the pornographic photographs and knew of the affair with Baron von Braun, although he had turned a blind eye to this for reasons of his own. Until now he had been prepared to let the marriage continue on her terms. He was a man of the world and, having lived for so long in France, he was willing to follow the French tradition of turning a blind eye to extra-marital relationships if they were carried on discreetly.

But when he was confronted with this dangerous, destructive, treacherous element of Margaret's character, the last straw broke the camel's back. The Duke might have wanted money from his wife, but he was not prepared to sacrifice his children for it. Everyone has their price, but he was not prepared to sell his soul and his honour.

'I think if I paid him off, and admitted to having an affair with *one* man, that I never had, which is in a way, perjury too! I mean, that's what he wanted. He wanted money and me to say that I'd had an affair with two men. He wanted to divorce me. He didn't want me to divorce him.

'I was determined to blow this thing sky high. Win or lose, I wasn't going to keep this all under cover for ever. I told him to go and jump in the lake, to take his petition, his lawyer and his gang, and *get*!'

The Duke was appalled when she told Thornton outright that the boys were illegitimate. 'He went straight to his lawyer, and said, "She's mentioned the unmentionable subject of the children *in front* of Air-Marshal Thornton." And they had me up for contempt of court. That's when the headlines came out, saying, "SHE'S GOING TO PRISON." I hadn't mentioned the damned children. I hadn't mentioned one word about them. It never came into the conversation. He went straight round to see Louise too, to say that I had talked about this to him. Air-Marshal Thornton refused to be involved, and therefore the thing actually fell to the ground.

'But there were no details about it in the press. The English newspapers don't print things about children. They're quite good about that. We had it heard in a very obscure court at Oxford. But, of course, everybody was wondering what the hell Louise Timpson was getting at me for, and it went badly against me.'

Margaret faced the motion to have her jailed under civil law in the High Court in London on 20 December 1959. It was listed in the official High Court list briefly as 'Timpson v. Argyll – Committal'. The application to Mr Justice Paull was for an order committing Margaret to prison for contempt of court. If successful, she would have been taken to HM Prison Holloway by the High Court tipstaff, Mr Wilfred Chambers. The subjects of the complaint – the Duke's heir, the Marquess of Lorne, aged twenty-two, was serving with the Argyll and Sutherland Highlanders as a subaltern in Germany and his younger brother, thirteen-year-old Lord Colin Campbell, was at school – could not be present in court.

Mr Justice Paull heard the application in chambers, held in camera, forbidding either the press or the public to attend the hearing which started at 10.30 a.m. Margaret arrived at the court at 2.20 p.m. She sat relaxed on a bench in the corridor for a few minutes puffing at a cigarette and went into the court at 2.45. She emerged four minutes later with her QC, Mr Gardiner, who conferred with her in a consulting room. They returned to their seats by the time Mr Justice Paull ordered the doors to be opened to the reporters at 3.14 p.m., and he gave a warning to the press about the publication of matters relating to the hearing. The judge said, 'In this matter I desire to state in open court that while I have been in chambers I have taken a certain course.' He forbade the press to mention what had been said in court.

Margaret left the court a free woman, but the court order hung over her head for the rest of her life: if she ever questioned the children's paternity again, she would be sent straight to prison.

As she climbed into her chauffeur-driven limousine wearing a black coat with brown mink collar, a cerise Breton sailor hat with black veil, and a triple string of perfectly matched pearls, she was asked whether she was happy or happier. She hesitated before answering for a moment, and then after a quick glance at her solicitor Mr Cecil Jobson, said, 'I am happy. I think I can say that, can't I?'

Earlier that month, September 1959, the Duke learnt that Margaret had intended having the street-door lock to her house changed. He telephoned his thirty-year-old daughter, Lady Jeanne Campbell, to say that he wanted to raid the house in an attempt to get hold of the vital diary and any supporting documents to be able to lodge his divorce petition. They let themselves into Margaret's house at 6 a.m. on 10 September, using the latch-key he still had, climbed the two flights of stairs to Margaret's bedroom where they found her asleep in bed, and unaccompanied. Then they stole back downstairs to the study which they methodically ransacked. Unable to find what they were looking for, they crept back up to her bedroom and tiptoed inside, not daring to breathe, to search for the diary.

The Duke looked round the room: the current four-year diary was lying on Margaret's bedside table. He snatched it up, rammed it into his overcoat pocket and gestured for his daughter to leave at once.

Margaret was terrified: 'I was fast asleep, and woke to hear drawers and cupboard doors being opened and shut in the study downstairs. Just as I reached out to switch on the bedside light, Ian and his daughter Jeanne came into my bedroom. I asked Ian what he wanted and told Jeanne to get out. But she rushed forward and held me down on the bed. I struggled, but I couldn't free myself. Ian then darted to my bedside, grabbed my private diary which was on the table beside me, and they scurried out of the house. Can you imagine going into someone's house when they're in bed upstairs and virtually holding a gun and grabbing the present diary I had?'

Later that morning the Duke, triumphant, lodged the diary with his solicitors, and then he and his daughter left for Inveraray Castle.

A week later Margaret received an injunction issuing a temporary prohibition restraining her from entering Inveraray Castle. It had been issued by Lord Wheatley, who, four years later, was to hear the Argylls' lengthy divorce case in the Edinburgh Court.

The Duke had stated in his application for the order against Margaret that he had instructed his solicitors to start divorce proceedings.

Margaret summoned her solicitors the same day, instructing them to issue a writ against Jeanne claiming damages for trespass. The Duke was perfectly entitled to enter the marital home but not so his daughter. Margaret claimed that Jeanne had gained unauthorized entry into her house and had seized her personal property. The terms of the writ were set in motion.

In May that year, on his return from Australia, the Duke had forbidden Margaret to enter Inveraray Castle; his recent application to the court alleged that,

Despite the prohibition, together with her father and stepmother, she visited Inveraray Castle on 12 May, and against the wishes of the petitioner, insisted on remaining for a few days.

On 3 September, without permission of and unknown to the petitioner, who was abroad at the time, she telephoned one of the servants at the castle, informing her that she was proposing to visit the castle for the weekend, but instructed the servant that she was on no account to inform the Duke's chamberlain of her proposed visit. During a further telephone conversation with a servant the Duchess said that she understood the petitioner would not be at the castle at the time of her proposed visit.

She arrived at Inveraray Castle on 5 September and immediately proceeded to the Duke's study and, finding it locked, requested the butler to hand her the keys. On being informed that the butler had already handed the keys to the chamberlain, who refused to allow the Duchess to have them, the Duchess instructed a local ironmonger to open the door of the study. He failed to open the door and the Duchess sent for a locksmith from Glasgow. He tried to open the door and left a key suitable for the door with the Duchess. It is believed that the key is still in the Duchess's possession.

She thereafter spent some time in the study and removed certain articles, including an oil painting, some photographs, and two boomerangs. She broke certain gramophone records belonging to the Duke and of which, as she was aware, he was particularly fond.

It is believed that her actions, particularly with regard to the records, were motivated by spite. She also attempted to enter the vaults of the castle and in order to do so tampered with the burglar alarm.

Before leaving the castle, she told a servant that she proposed returning at the end of that month, and the day after the Duke removed the diary from her bedroom in

London, she told him that she planned to return to the castle to take up residence about 18 or 20 September, within ten days.

The Duke forbade her to return to the castle, but despite the prohibition, she sent him the following telegram:

ARRIVING CASTLE FOR LUNCH SATURDAY 19TH
WITH MY FATHER AND DONALD NICHOLL STOP
ANOTHER COUPLE ARRIVING FOR DINNER AND
WEEKEND STOP PLEASE INFORM STAFF AND TELL
MACDONALD TO MAKE SURE MY BEDROOM IS QUITE
READY STOP GIVE MY FONDEST LOVE AND A BIG
KISS TO COLIN STOP MARGARET

The Duke sent a telegram in reply.

I CONFIRM THAT YOU ARE FORBIDDEN TO ENTER
INVERARAY CASTLE

and suspecting that she would ignore his order, applied for the injunction to ban her.

Less than a month later, Margaret visited the castle for four hours after applying to the Edinburgh Court for access so that she could collect her belongings. Mr Fraser, QC for Margaret, had asked for the injunction to be revoked, claiming that many of the valuable furnishings, tapestries and pictures were her property, having been given to her by the Duke by Deed of Gift some time before in exchange for funds to restore the castle. But in fact the Duke had no right to dispose of the precious items as they were held in trust and not his to give. She said their married life had become unhappy because of the Duke's excessive drinking and behaviour both in public and private, claiming that once the Duke violently assaulted her, causing her pain.

On 22 October Margaret, accompanied by two legal representatives and her maid toured the castle, followed by the Duke, his son Lord Lorne, and the Duke's legal representative. 'It was a farcical day,' the Duke reported. 'Margaret toured the whole castle, sweeping through room after room pointing apparently at random to pieces of old furniture, Campbell family portraits and even suits of armour, "That's mine – that's mine, too," she kept saying.' Gently her advisers persuaded her that she must be mistaken.

She returned to London a broken woman. She had never much cared for life at Inveraray, but this visit had been a bitter blow to her pride. She who had always been in control now realized that she would have to let go. Yet she could not do so. It was not in her nature. The events that had occurred changed her life and her routine. She was confused and worried about the future. For once, she felt vulnerable. She was sure that she had lost her husband, but not so sure that she was not losing her reasoning as well.

In fact two vans carried away all that she was allowed to take – her clothes, linen and personal effects. But she had been cheated of the precious spoils she had been led to believe were hers.

CHAPTER SEVEN

Into the Breach

B Y the time he had reached twenty, Margaret's son Brian had become one of London society's most eligible bachelors. His mother was an heiress, his father, Charles Sweeny, a successful merchant banker, his sister was a duchess with two stately homes and his stepfather was a duke. His father had set up a sizeable trust for him and his sister. However, he had failed his preliminary examination at Oxford – he was one of the youngest scholars reading modern languages at Christ Church. He took the examination again the following term. 'I am in hot water with my family,' he told a friend at the time. 'Frances and Mummy are hardly speaking to me. I have been blamed for living it up too much at Oxford.'

In July 1959, at the time of Margaret's attempt to implicate her in the MacPherson affair and the 'child from Venice' scheme, Diana Napier announced to friends that she had found a suitable bride for Margaret's son, but this was speculation rather than fact, besides which Margaret was far too occupied with legal matters to contemplate vetting her handsome dark-haired son's prospective wives. In the event, after he gained second-class honours in his Oxford finals second time round, his father sent him to America to take a course at the Harvard Business School.

Although Margaret's octogenarian father and fifty-six-year-old stepmother had seemed to be happily married ever since they left Caxton Hall three years earlier in 1956, George Whigham left his wife and moved into the mews cottage that was part of Margaret's house in Upper Grosvenor Street after a matrimonial tiff at Linacres, their Berkshire country home. Jane, however, joined him on occasion when she visited London.

Margaret had always been close to her father and as an only child leant heavily on him both emotionally and financially. Although her father had made over 5 per cent of his capital to her every year, she was always overdrawn at her bank and her father always had to settle up. He had, after all, encouraged the lifestyle she had chosen, and in which she revelled, and he enjoyed the kudos of having a beautiful, elegant daughter with the elevated social status of a duchess.

But aside from Margaret's resentment of him sharing his life and fortune with another woman, she needed to find a new way of discrediting the Duke, who had filed his petition for divorce. Margaret's infidelities and the poison-pen letters that cast doubt on his sons' paternity made him realize that he had married a monster. Margaret knew she had to counter-petition, naming at least one woman. The target of her hare-brained scheme was her stepmother. With this plan she imagined she could kill two birds with one stone.

Jane Whigham complained at first that Margaret was trying to ruin her marriage but matters grew worse. 'At first the Duchess and I got along splendidly,' said Jane. 'We often chatted over the telephone and sometimes when I was in London she would invite me over for tea at Argyll House.'

By August 1959, Jane noticed that she was being followed. Detectives waited day and night across the road from the flat where she joined her estranged husband in Margaret's mews. 'They followed my blue Hillman car to restaurants or when I visited a woman friend and then followed me home again. A fortnight ago I dialled 999 and had both detectives removed from outside the flat by police. But they soon returned.' Jane had wisely made a careful note of the car number of the detectives trailing her, and through her own detective work she discovered that they were employed by Margaret.

Back at their country home, Jane tackled her husband about his daughter's conduct and when he told her that he proposed to do nothing about it, a fight ensued between them. She claimed in an interview later that she ended up with a black eye and a bruised fist, and he, licking his wounds, retreated to his daughter for sanctuary.

Hurt at the way she had been hounded and now physically harmed, instead of taking legal action, Jane reported the incidents to the press who willingly printed her complaints. But a week later her husband, at Margaret's behest, issued a statement through his solicitors refuting the allegations his wife had made against him, categorically denying 'that his daughter has in any way tried to upset or interfere with his marriage; on the contrary,' the statement continued, 'she has always been on the best of terms with his wife until recently, and accepted her stepmother with pleasure as a member of the family.'

A few months later Whigham asked Jane to sign a deed of separation agreement upon which he would pay her £20,000 in settlement. He also promised that once she had signed it he would visit her frequently at their marital home in Berkshire and make over to her more money on each occasion. She had reservations about this arrangement, not wanting to feel like a mere mistress, but signed the document, understanding that he wanted to show it to Margaret as proof that they had really parted.

Six months later Margaret and her father spent January and February 1960 holidaying in the Bahamas where she discovered that he had contracted cancer of the throat. In September that year Whigham received a visitor at Margaret's house, clutching a letter. It was a writ. Jane was suing for divorce eighteen months after they had married on grounds of cruelty. He was eighty years old, with two months to live. Shortly after Jane heard of his illness she offered to withdraw the divorce petition on compassionate grounds, which he declined to Margaret's delight as she wanted to free herself, her father and his estate from this interloper. Two weeks later when Jane telephoned, the butler had been instructed to tell her that her husband was out. He was, in fact, in the London Clinic, heavily sedated. 'I suspected this,' said Jane, 'so I disguised my voice, pretending to be someone else, a woman the butler knew, and telephoned again. This time, taken in by the pretence, he said, "Oh, madam, didn't you know Mr Whigham is in the Clinic and they don't expect him to live the night?"'

Jane and her mother rushed up to the London Clinic in Devonshire Place from Berkshire. When she asked to see her husband she was told that she could not because the doctors were with him. She was taken to a small waiting room and offered tea, which she declined. She wanted only to see her dying husband, probably for the last time. She did not know that the hospital staff had been instructed by Margaret not to allow her to see him. Then, a member of staff telephoned Margaret to tell her that her stepmother had arrived in a distressed condition. Margaret was also told that her father's life was coming to a close.

Margaret summoned her chauffeur and raced over to the Clinic. In her panic she pushed Jane aside and headed towards her father's room. She put her chauffeur on guard outside the door to prevent Jane from following her in. Moments later Jane heard a shriek. It was Margaret's voice.

Jane knew he was dead.

'Margaret came out and said to me in a tone so venomous that it made me shudder: "Get out! You will never see my father again, alive or dead."'

With that, Margaret swept out, followed by her chauffeur and leaving Jane bereft. The doctor moved towards Jane and confirmed that her husband had died. In lowered tones the matron told her that she could go into his room after they had cleared it up. But she had no wish to do so. It was too late. She wanted to remember him as he had been.

Margaret arranged the funeral and Jane received a letter from her late husband's solicitors forbidding her to attend the service. But she went along to the Golders Green crematorium all the same, sat in the traditional widow's pew and left shortly after the cremation, escorted by her brother.

Jane contested her husband's English will, but achieved nothing as she had already been provided with the £20,000 settlement. Although he had also cut her out of the will relating to his house and land in the Bahamas, she was able to claim a dower right under an old Nassau law.

In the end Jane triumphed over Margaret if not over her late husband. She was awarded £25,000 damages against her, plus costs, in a libel action she brought against Margaret who had named her as co-respondent in the divorce action she had brought against the Duke.

By 1963 Margaret had paid out over £100,000 in claims of libel and slander brought against her, including the costs and damages in the Duke's divorce petition. There were also other actions which were to cost her dearly in the fullness of time.

Up until May 1960 while she and her father had been enjoying the warmth of the Bahamas Margaret had been involved in so many legal actions that it was almost beyond her lawyers to keep track of them. The petitions and cross-petitions included the Duke and Margaret's divorce actions against each other, Margaret suing her stepdaughter Lady Jeanne Campbell for trespass on her premises, her step-mother suing Margaret, and the pending action of her former social secretary, who was suing her for libel and slander. The Duke's former wife, Mrs Robert Timpson's, action had been satisfied before Christmas in 1959. Action was also being taken against her for entering Inveraray Castle illegally and seizing objects not belonging to her and Margaret counter-claiming that various valuable items had been passed to her by the Duke as Deed of Gift. On 2 and 3 May the worst of it happened when Margaret's former secretary Yvonne MacPherson won her three-year libel and slander action with Margaret having to pay £7,000 damages plus costs. To understand Mrs MacPherson's claim against Margaret it is essential to refer to the incidents that had taken place three years before, as a run-up to the High Court action. The chronology has been interwoven with so many legal actions, writs, claims, counter-claims, accusations and denials that Margaret, whose sense of reasoning was lim-ited, must have been confused. She had, however, enlisted the services of the best solicitors and barristers available.

The marriage had come to an end and the Duke moved out of Margaret's house in early 1957 to stay at Claridge's where he took a suite; it was less than five minutes' walk from the house. He was prepared to spend time with her during the day, and to dine with her occasionally, but made it a strict rule always to return to his own bed at the hotel by night.

'The only person he would see and talk to at that time was my ex-secretary Mrs Yvonne MacPherson,' Margaret said. 'After a while, Ian insisted on going to Paris alone. I had no idea when he would return to me, if ever. But a few days later he sent for me to join him. I went immediately and found him looking thin, distressed and ill. I knew that he had been taking drinamyl tablets [purple hearts] and the first thing I did when I saw him was to make him promise not to take any more.'

Margaret returned home and the Duke went back to Claridge's.

Amongst Margaret's friends at the time were a handful of women who were both her confidantes and equally close friends of the Duke. She involved them in the libel action of Mrs MacPherson, which took place over the next three years before it finally came before the Queen's Bench Division in May 1960. The women were called as witnesses and all spoke against Margaret in the action.

Mrs MacPherson was the widow of a brigadier who had served with the Duke in the Argyll and Sutherlands and had spent five years with him in the prisoner-of-war camp. She also worked as social secretary for Maureen, Marchioness of Dufferin and Ava, a Guinness heiress, who lived in one of the largest houses in Knightsbridge, London. The Marchioness and Margaret had been friends of many years' standing and Mrs MacPherson worked for Margaret in the mornings and for the Marchioness in the afternoons. Since Margaret no longer had much practical work for her, Mrs MacPherson had begun to work for the Duke instead.

In three different actions, Mrs MacPherson claimed that the Duchess had slandered her. Apparently Margaret had telephoned the Duke's doctor and a mutual friend of theirs, Mrs Magda Buchel, to say that Mrs MacPherson had been spreading malicious rumours saying that the Duke had moved out of Margaret's house because their marriage was on the rocks. Margaret had also said that Mrs MacPherson had been paid by the press for information about the state of their marriage, and had mentioned Lord Rothermere as her source of information.

Mrs MacPherson also claimed that Margaret had told Mrs Buchel that she was in danger of losing her job because of her indiscretions. She was still employed by the Marchioness, who denied threatening her with dismissal.

Magda Buchel, a cousin of the Duke of Norfolk, had been a close friend of Margaret for a long time and was called to give evidence in support of Mrs MacPherson's complaints. In the action presided over by Mr Justice Donovan before a jury on 3 May 1960, Magda Buchel swore under oath that in May 1956 Margaret had told her that 'Mrs MacPherson is shortly to be dismissed from her appointment with the Marchioness and her husband Judge John Maude because they had found out about her disloyalty to Ian and myself.' Still on oath, she testified that in January 1957 Margaret told her on the telephone that 'Mrs MacPherson is spreading the rumour that my husband and I have parted and that is why he has moved to Claridge's. Various members of the press have told me so.' She admitted that Margaret had told the Duke's doctor, Dr Petro, the same story.

On 25 February 1957 Magda Buchel had paid Margaret a visit at Upper Grosvenor Street where she confronted her with the slanders, imploring her to withdraw them, to which Margaret replied: 'I refuse to withdraw anything. Yvonne knows perfectly well she has been paid for giving information to the press. Lord Rothermere told me that. She has been employed by his newspaper group for years and gets £20 every time she opens her mouth.'

Worse was to come. Mrs MacPherson claimed that on 18 April 1957, Margaret had sent a telegram to the Duke. It was telephoned through from Inveraray post office, purporting to have been sent by her, Mrs MacPherson.

It read:

Duke of Argyll, Inveraray Castle, Argyll

RUSHING OFF FOR TEN DAYS' LEAVE BUT ALL IS READY AS WE PLANNED TO TEAR STRIPS OFF MARGARET FINANCIALLY AND OTHERWISE STOP A MILLION THANKS FOR YOUR LOVE, SUPPORT AND INVALUABLE INFORMATION WITHOUT WHICH I WOULD BE HELPLESS STOP HAPPY EASTER AND THEN INTO BATTLE SIDE BY SIDE STOP YVONNE

She alleged that those words meant that she and the Duke were acting in collusion with the purpose of humiliating and extorting money from Margaret. In her defence, Margaret denied sending the damaging document or that it was defamatory.

Mrs MacPherson's son Rory, who became a well-known television reporter, testified that on 18 April, the date of the telegram, he had left home at about 10.45 a.m. for Putney. If his mother had telephoned a telegram that morning he would have known about it. He knew, without doubt, that she had not sent it.

The Duke, who appeared as a witness for Mrs MacPherson, told the court that he had filed a petition for divorce from Margaret six months before this hearing. He also explained that he had moved into a hotel because the situation at home had become intolerable. When asked by counsel about supplying Mrs MacPherson with documents which would be useful ammunition for her to have against his wife, he admitted: 'I supplied Mrs MacPherson with all the documents in my possession which may be useful to her in her action against my wife.' Under cross-examination he also admitted that he had called Margaret 'a yellow belly', and that he had referred to her in a letter as 'S' which meant 'Satan'. His reference to her as 'Satan' came after he had talked about a letter he had sent to Mrs MacPherson at Claridge's in March 1957 while he and Margaret were on holiday in Siena, Italy. Mrs MacPherson did secretarial work for him there, but had not seen the letter at that time. He told the court that on their return to London Margaret had stolen the letter from the postbox at the hotel or from the porter. It said: 'My dear Yvonne. You were right. "M" took the bait and relayed the message within hours.' 'M' referred to Margaret. When asked what he meant by the word 'bait', he replied: 'It might have been written by me with diabolical subtlety to catch out one more lie on behalf of my wife.'

Dr John Petro of Montagu Square was next to be called to give evidence. He said that he had been ordered to do so by the court under subpoena. He was a friend of the Duke as well as his medical attendant. He also knew Margaret and was acquainted with her voice. He remembered being asked on the telephone to visit the Duke at Claridge's in January 1957, and that shortly after, on the same day, Margaret had telephoned asking him to see the Duke about some pills he had prescribed. She had also said that Mrs MacPherson, her ex-secretary, had been informing members of the press that she and the Duke had parted. He had replied that he had great doubts that that could be so. He had then visited the Duke and had heard the same slander repeated on the telephone by Margaret. Dr Petro had overheard the conversation between them. When he called on Mrs MacPherson on 4 March, he repeated the conversation and she was extremely upset. Questioned about a doctor's confidentiality between himself and his patients, Dr Petro admitted that: 'When I was confronted with Mrs MacPherson in a terrible state over these dreadful rumours, I did mention to her that they were exactly what I had heard on two occasions over the telephone.'

Continuing her evidence in support of Mrs MacPherson's claim, Mrs Buchel told the court that she remembered a conversation with Margaret in the spring of 1957. It was about the relationship between Mrs MacPherson, who worked for the Marchioness of Dufferin and Ava, and the Marchioness's husband, Judge Maude.

The heiress Maureen Guinness, now in her eighties, was a much sought-after society figure. She was beautiful, witty and won a reputation for having a rather sharp tongue. During the thirties she also won the hand of the Marquess of Dufferin and Ava. After his death, she married the tall, charming judge John Maude. He, too, was witty, with a naughty twinkle in his eye. Even though she remarried, Lady Dufferin was determined to be addressed by her old title and became known officially as Maureen, Marchioness of Dufferin and Ava, never as Mrs John Maude.

Magda Buchel continued that Margaret had put it about that Lady Dufferin and Judge Maude were not satisfied with Mrs MacPherson as they had discovered that she had been disloyal to them. She said that they would sack her because of it. Magda Buchel added that she knew this to be untrue because Lady Dufferin and Judge Maude, who were friends of hers, had told her that they were, indeed, satisfied with Mrs MacPherson and her work.

Margaret had also told Magda Buchel later that Mrs MacPherson had given information to the press regarding a rift in her marriage, saying that because of this the Duke had gone to live at Claridge's. Margaret had also told her that Mrs MacPherson had been seen by the hall porter gossiping to the press about them. Mrs Buchel continued that on her visit to Margaret of 25 February, Margaret refused to withdraw anything she had said about Mrs MacPherson and had added yet another slander, this time with regard to Lord Rothermere. Mrs Buchel said she had become quite nervous about Margaret then and had said to her, 'For God's sake, don't go on saying things like that. It will get you into trouble.' She reported that the Duke had also said, 'Margaret, won't you listen to your best friend?' But Margaret had replied, 'I don't listen to anybody.'

Magda Buchel said that Margaret had told her on another occasion that she had found a most interesting telegram under the Duke's blotter at Inveraray Castle, and relayed the contents of it to her. She added that it was impossible to think that Mrs MacPherson could have sent such a telegram and Margaret had replied that she knew it had come from her because it had her telephone number on it.

In cross-examination Mrs Buchel said that after Mrs MacPherson had heard from the Duke in Scotland about receiving the telegram she came round to her, Mrs Buchel's, home, rang the doorbell and handed her a piece of paper saying: 'Magda, this is the telegram I am supposed to have sent. But it was sent by your friend the Duchess.'

Mrs MacPherson told the court that she wrote to Margaret the following day reproaching her for accusing her of sending the telegram. But the next day, before Margaret had received Mrs MacPherson's letter, Mrs MacPherson received a telephone call from her. She was surprised to hear from the Duchess because she knew that Margaret could not have had her letter by then.

'I asked her why she had used my name in some fantastic story. I didn't begin to understand. She wanted me to say that I had told her about the telegram, but I was very firm. I wouldn't do it. How could I? I was very angry about her using my name. And then Margaret became very upset, and cried a lot. I was frankly very sorry for her. She asked me to forgive her for having used my name, and I said I would.'

The friendship between the two women continued, since Mrs MacPherson had agreed to forgive her, and when they met over Easter the matter was not mentioned again. But, unknown to Mrs MacPherson at the time, Margaret

continued her campaign to discredit her, and in the end
Mrs MacPherson had no alternative but to sue her.

Earlier, Mrs MacPherson had said in the witness box
that when Margaret sought her advice about her domestic
affairs she told her that it would be a good thing if she did
not continue going out in the evenings with male friends.
She also suggested that she should stop making derogatory
remarks to the Duke about the Campbell clan.

The next witness to give evidence for Mrs MacPherson
was Diana Napier. She told the court that she had known
Margaret since 1935 or 1936 and the Duke for about two
years. She had never met or spoken to Mrs MacPherson
until she saw her at the court the previous day. She explained
that she had lost touch with Margaret for a time, because
when her husband, Richard Tauber, died she had been left
in difficult financial circumstances, and had decided not to
see any of her friends until she could 'stand them a lunch
in return for a lunch'.

She said that she received a telephone call from Margaret
in the spring of 1959: 'She asked me if I would make a statement to the effect that I was talking to her on the telephone
for twenty minutes on a morning in 1957, and I refused.
I asked her, "What is it all about?" and she said, "I'm being
accused of sending a telegram, but I didn't do it." She didn't
say any more about it then and said that she would tell me
about it when she saw me.'

They met towards the end of July 1959: 'She [Margaret] was in a very nervous state. She told me that she'd been asked to sign an affidavit, swearing that she hadn't sent a telegram. She said she would have to do it, unless she could stall until she got back from America, adding, "I must have been very mad, and very silly, but I did send it." I told her that she must telephone her solicitor and tell him the truth. She said that she was going to see Tony Marreco, who is a lawyer. I told her that he would tell her the same thing. I told her to confess because it would be perjury. I later had dinner with her on 7 September and she told me that she had signed the affidavit, and I said, "How terrible." She said, "Everyone's ganging up on me, and I've got to fight back." I agreed that if she was in the right she should fight.'

Diana Napier was subsequently contacted by Mrs MacPherson's solicitors and asked to give evidence. In cross-examination, Mr Gardiner, for Margaret's defence, asked her, 'The first time you were asked to recollect all these matters was last Thursday?' Yes. 'On the first occasion that the subject arose, the Duchess told you that she had not sent the telegram?'

'Yes, the first time.'

'And I suggest it was the same the second time?'

'I have no reason to be here. I don't like it,' said Diana. 'But I can't go through life having it on my conscience that a perfect stranger suffered because I gave false evidence.'

After the midday adjournment, Mr Gardiner told his lordship that on his advice, given after careful consideration, Margaret would not be calling any evidence. She had thrown in the towel.

Addressing the jury, counsel for Mrs MacPherson, Mr Gilbert Beyfus, QC, said that in view of the course taken they would have to find a verdict in her favour, for whatever amount of damages they thought appropriate. On the first matter, Margaret admitted that she had slandered Mrs MacPherson by saying that she was in danger of losing her job. Magda Buchel had repeated the slander to Mrs MacPherson so that she knew exactly what Margaret had said. The jury would also have to consider what, if any, damage Mrs MacPherson had sustained and what was the appropriate sum for something said to a very old friend, a *confidante*, and repeated to her. It was proved that Margaret had slandered her in the matter regarding the telegram. But they could not claim slander for anything said by her in front of the Duke. In law any wife can say what she likes to her husband and any husband can say what he likes to his wife without fear of legal action.

Back to the telegram, Beyfus said that the jury, having heard the evidence on both sides, would no doubt agree that the telegram had been sent by Margaret. It was a case where a woman, however stupidly, had sent a telegram in someone else's name, to her own husband only; and the only publication alleged was to the post office clerks. In that event the jury would award Mrs MacPherson such damages as they thought right to compensate her for any damage to her reputation in the eyes of those post office clerks.

'To say, as Mrs MacPherson has done, that the clerk who took down the telegram would look up all sorts of directories to see who "Margaret" and "Yvonne" were was not right, though it might be more accurate to say that somebody in the village might have put two and two together.' He said that it was a case in which the only slander was to Magda Buchel. She was a friend of long standing and still very friendly with Mrs MacPherson. In substance, she had never believed a word of the slander. Dr Petro, the doctor to both parties, who also said he did not believe the slander, was still friendly with Mrs MacPherson and was still her doctor.

The judge now referred to the post office clerks in the case of the telegram. He believed that Mrs MacPherson had not suffered any substantial loss of reputation through the publication of the telegram. He believed that it would never have reached these proportions if it had not been for the Duke's interest in the matter. This item in the slander action should not be met with extravagant damages.

Beyfus said that the jury had probably been astonished that after a fight that had gone on for three years, Margaret had resisted every effort to induce her to withdraw the accusations she was making against Mrs MacPherson. Yet when she had realized the strength of the evidence against her, Margaret had refused to go into the witness box and face the music. He said that it must have been a terrible shock to Diana Napier to have to give evidence as she had. Margaret had admitted to her last July that she had sent the telegram to the Duke. Also, in September, she had admitted that to try to escape the consequences she had committed perjury. That had been why Margaret had refused to go into the witness box. She knew that she had been lying.

The jury should remember the wicked story about Lord Rothermere, he added. If there had been a vestige of truth in it the legal representative for Margaret could have called Lord Rothermere to give evidence. But there was not an iota of truth in it. It was the invention of an utterly malicious mind. Margaret, through her solicitors, said that she was only trying to see where the truth lay. The telegram was a concoction which she, 'in her evil mind', developed in the hope that this story of her husband, in which he had banded together with his secretary against his wife, would be spread throughout the village. The case of the telegram was one of machination after machination, plot after plot, excuse after excuse, contrivance after contrivance, the judge added. What sort of punishment should fall on a woman who had been as wicked as Margaret in this case? To this moment, the judge went on, not one single word of apology, not one single word of regret had been shown by her.

Mr Gardiner (acting for Margaret) had addressed the jury in a short pronouncement. No doubt he was glad to sit down as quickly as he could. He had not, apparently, been able to get Margaret to authorize him to express one syllable of regret for the suffering to which she had put Mrs MacPherson over the last three years.

The jury might consider whether this was not a case in which their verdict should be one to punish her. The jury were asked to recall Beyfus, for Mrs MacPherson, making his opening statement the day before, when he said that: 'When one contemplated the Duchess of Argyll, one thinks back to the fairy tales one learned in one's youth, when all the good fairies assembled at a christening and showered their gifts on the infant. But one's imagination recalls that in some of those fairy tales there were bad fairies who had not been invited to the christening, but who came and said, "I can't recall all the gifts which have been showered on the child, but I will give the infant my own gift. You shall grow up to be a poisonous liar." There imagination ceases and reality begins. If you believe the evidence Mrs MacPherson will give, and that tendered on her behalf, that has happened, and the Duchess of Argyll has become, and is, a poisonous liar.'

In summing up, his lordship said that on the slanders it was enough if Mrs MacPherson had proved that the substance of the words pleaded was uttered, and the jury might think that it was not now disputed that she had proved that. On the libel, the law had always regarded telegrams as being published to the clerk in the post office who had to hear them. It might be that at the London end of this particular telegram nobody bothered to find out who 'Yvonne' was and perhaps did not care. But at the other end, and no one had suggested that Scotland was any different from England for this purpose of publication, many people, seeing that a telegram had come to the Duke, would know quite well who 'Margaret' was and might also know the identity of 'Yvonne'. They might think very much the less of Mrs MacPherson if they thought she had sent a telegram of this kind, indicating that she was in hostile league with the Duke against his wife to do his wife some injury.

The question was what the damages should be. The jury should give such sum for the four slanders as they thought would reasonably compensate Mrs MacPherson for the wrong done to her. They should take into account the absence of any apology or retraction down to this moment, as also that the only persons to whom the slanders were published were Mrs Buchel and Dr Petro, who were still friends of Mrs MacPherson. Against that, they must take into account any damage likely to happen in the future from the slanders that some future employers might think, 'There is never any smoke without a fire,' despite the result of a court action. So far as Mrs MacPherson's vocation was concerned it was difficult to imagine anything more serious to say of a confidential secretary than that she was willing to sell her late employers' secrets for money and had been in the pay of a newspaper group for years. The jury should assess one figure in respect of the four slanders and a separate figure in respect of the libel.

The jury retired at 3.15 p.m. and returned at 4 p.m. They awarded £2,500 for the slanders and £4,500 for the libel. Judgment was accordingly entered for Mrs MacPherson for £7,000 and costs.

Tall and slim, wearing a black coat and skirt, a triple row of pearls and a close-fitting brown and white straw hat, Mrs MacPherson smiled jubilantly as she left the court, and said, 'How relieved I am that it is all over and done with. My name has now been completely cleared. I just cannot believe after three years that the enormous cloud has suddenly lifted. I simply cannot take it in.' Regarding her plans for the future she explained that she would not be retiring to the country but would go on doing the work that she loved.

Outside the court, the Duke said to the Marchioness, 'You lost your bet. You owe me four shillings.' She smiled, dipped into her handbag and handed him two florins. He had bet her that the case would not go on after that day.

After she had given evidence, Diana Napier had walked to her seat and burst into tears. A few minutes later, still sobbing, she had left with two friends. 'I am being converted to the Roman Catholic faith,' she said. 'When I heard that I was to be called in court I spoke to my priest and he told me that I must tell nothing but the truth. That is what I have done today.' She also was back in court when the jury returned. As she heard their verdict she whispered, 'This is horrible. It is terrible. This is a dreadful day.' She and Margaret never met again.

After the hearing had drawn to a close, Margaret sat, a lone figure in the courtroom, while mink-coated and bejewelled socialites crowded round to congratulate Mrs MacPherson. Wearing a red straw boater with a velvet band and a black veil, a grey and white chequered coat and skirt, she had written notes with a gold pencil and often referred to a loose-leaf diary. Before the end of this High Court action, which had taken three years to come to court and cost her £7,000 plus £3,500 costs, she had already paid out over £10,000 in libel and legal costs, arising from the paternity suit which had been heard in camera at the High Court five months before, and also involved the Duke and Mrs MacPherson. 'It's a bad defeat,' she said of this last case. 'It is heart-breaking. Right up to that time I was willing to fight all the way. I wouldn't have gone to court in the first place if I didn't believe I had a first-class chance of winning.

The decision to offer no evidence from me was reached during the luncheon adjournment,' on the advice of her legal representatives.

The MacPherson case was only the second of many that Margaret lost, to her great cost both morally and financially.

No one could have been more triumphant over Margaret's defeat than an erstwhile close friend. Maureen, Marchioness of Dufferin and Ava, was a well-known figure in both social and theatre circles and an amusing intimate of Sir Noël Coward. She was a contemporary of Margaret's and vied in the thirties with her beauty and social standing. An oil painting of her by Augustus John, at the height of her beauty with long Titian hair, looked down from the wall on the staircase in her home leading from the hall up to her drawing room. This was surrounded by other famous works of art including a Boucher and a Canaletto.

Still witty and sparkling, she now had bleached wavy hair on top of which hats sat rather precariously. Equipped with a deep husky voice and a quick, gurgling laugh, she was known for the huge Irish linen rag-bag that accompanied her wherever she went. It contained, among other goodies, an assortment of portable necessities including pills and funny letters from friends which she would enjoy reading to all and sundry and amusing 'tricks', for which she would reach down at the most inappropriate moment. On one occasion at dinner in her elegant Knightsbridge dining room, she produced from it a tinted-tin erect phallus, which when wound up hopped about the pudding plates, the guests squealing in shocked delight. They loved her eccentricity and expected nothing less from this endearing friend. She was philanthropic to a fault, and had converted an old oast-house ('Maureen's Oast') in Lamberhurst, Kent, which was close to her own small country retreat, for arthritis sufferers, complete with ramps for wheelchairs and those on sticks.

It was she who had encouraged Mrs MacPherson, in whom she had the utmost faith and trust, to bring the action against Margaret, and had also guaranteed her legal costs through the three-year battle that culminated in her successful High Court action. After the case, Mrs MacPherson continued to work for her and John Maude.

Lady Dufferin's house in Knightsbridge had a high glass roof in one area which looked like a combination between a conservatory and a loft. After her husband had died, Lady Dufferin continued to live her usual lifestyle, and, amusing as ever, entertained her friends in the usual way. Moira Lister returned from a journey abroad, and was asked to dinner. 'I had been away and didn't know John had died,' Moira Lister says.

'Maureen and I were in her bedroom after dinner. That house has a sort of loft with a glass ceiling, and I said, "How is darling John?" She replied, "Oh, he's gone aloft." So I said,

"Could I go up and see him?" And she said, "I don't think so, dear."

Although Moira Lister and Margaret remained close friends, the Marchioness and Margaret never spoke again. Margaret, however, became a good friend of Maureen's son, himself married to another Guinness millionairess. Years later when he was disfigured by Kaposi's sarcoma (an Aids-related skin cancer) she crossed a room at a gala at the National Portrait Gallery and embraced him on both cheeks – he was a friend and there was nothing to be afraid of. Thereafter people were less reticent to shake his hand or talk to him. She had made her point.

'Ian was like a spider,' Margaret said. 'He got all these people working for him. Yvonne MacPherson, my own secretary, then there was Magda Buchel. She needed me. I didn't need her. Diana Tauber, Maureen Dufferin and then Mrs Timpson, his second wife. There were five of them including Ian. I always thought he would go too far, and he *did* go too far.'

Earlier in 1960, during Margaret's absence in the Bahamas, her solicitors had managed to settle her action claiming damages for trespass into her home by Lady Jeanne Campbell when she and the Duke seized the vital four-year diary that was to become an important part of his evidence in his divorce action against Margaret. An out-of-court admission and settlement of a negligible sum was paid by Lady Jeanne.

In June the Duke's divorce action was adjourned for twenty-eight days in Edinburgh Court of Session after a dispute about the Duke's misconduct allegations against Margaret. 'Two at least of these chapters of adultery are alleged to have taken place at a time when the parties were still cohabiting,' Mr C. E. Jauncey, acting for Margaret, said. 'The Duke alleges three chapters of adultery against the Duchess.' In effect, he had cited three different men, but had named specifically only two. Mr Peter Maxwell, for the Duke, referred to the pornographic photographs he had in his possession as evidence, but had declined to describe them fully. 'It would have been contrary to the best interests of our opponents,' Mr Maxwell said. 'I think it is a rather distasteful and wholly unnecessary thing to do.'

Margaret now realized the strength of the Duke's divorce action against her and that it would take at least another two years to come to court in Edinburgh. In a hasty attempt to divorce *him*, Margaret cross-petitioned in August, which was when she cited her stepmother as having had an adulterous affair with the Duke. It became clear to Jane Whigham for the first time why Margaret had had her followed by two detectives: it was an attempt to frame her and the Duke. 'This allegation is monstrous,' Jane protested. 'I have a complete defence.' The Duke also confirmed that it was a monstrous lie and that he, too, would be defending the allegation.

Having filed her petition, Margaret began to organize Brian's twenty-first birthday party although his birthday was not until the following April. He was due, however, to leave for the Harvard Business School. She arranged dinner for seventy guests at Claridge's on 1 October, and five hundred more joined the dance afterwards. The guests included Brian's sister Frances and the Duke of Rutland, the Duke and Duchess of Bedford, the Duke and Duchess of Sutherland, J. Paul Getty, the beautiful young Henrietta Tiarks, the year's outstanding débutante, and subsequently 'the bride of the year' when she married the Duke of Bedford's son and heir-apparent, the Marquess of Tavistock, movie stars including Douglas Fairbanks Jnr, who was to figure so prominently in Margaret's divorce case, Gary Cooper, Ray Milland and a string of other luminaries together with their respective wives and mistresses. She also flew Jean Sablon over from Paris for the cabaret spot and the guests swooned at the heart-throb crooning French love songs.

At the end of the year Margaret decided to spend a few weeks in New York visiting her son, then to travel on to South America, first to Buenos Aires then to Rio for the Carnival, on to Caracas, Venezuela, and finally the Bahamas to see the trustees about her father's Nassau will before returning to New York *en route* for London.

When she arrived in New York before setting off on her two-month journey, she received a telephone call from a hire-car company offering her preferential rates for a car and driver. He seemed anxious to use her name as a client for advertising purposes, and Margaret agreed to his low rates. She had not, however, bargained for the vehicle that turned up – a black Cadillac limousine wired with eaves-dropping equipment. The driver, Horace Schmahl, turned out to be a private detective working for the International Security Bureau, who, when indicted by a grand jury in New York, admitted that his services had been retained by a firm acting for solicitors in Britain, 'in connection with a matrimonial action'. Although the Duke had sought to obtain further evidence in support of his divorce action, Margaret could hardly have thought that he would go to such lengths. She had used the services of the hire-car company on three previous occasions: once on a journey to the airport, another with her son Brian, and the third with one of her Bahamas trustees, Sir Charles Russell, on a tour of New York. It was he who spotted the bugging device, which he had at first taken to be the air-conditioner at the back of the car.

After he was arrested at his Manhattan offices, Schmahl pleaded not guilty and was released on bail of £357.

Margaret sued him for £178,000, alleging he had installed the microphone and recorder in the car. But the New York Supreme Court decided that since she had suffered neither tangible harm nor legal injury, as a result of the eavesdropping, she had no case. She lost her claim and yet again was obliged to pay costs. Afterwards, Schmahl wrote Margaret a letter of apology for the inconvenience in recording the – as it turned out – incomprehensible tapes, assuring her that when she used his services again in the future the vehicle would be free of any bugging device.

Relentless in her pursuit of anyone who crossed her path Margaret won substantial damages from Associated Newspapers in March 1961 claiming libel in an article in Paul Tanfield's column in the *Daily Mail* of 20 January. Mr Helenus Milmo, acting for Margaret, said the action related to a report headlined 'Whigham's Widow in Will Claim'. The article clearly conveyed that, according to Mrs Whigham, while in the Bahamas the Duchess had circulated a wicked lie concerning her to prejudice Mrs Whigham's claim against her late husband's executors. Milmo contended that there was no truth whatever in Jane Whigham's statement, the facts being that under a deed of 1 August 1960, she and her husband had not merely separated but that she had received £20,000 on signing the deed. Also, during their marriage, she had received from him gifts to the value of approximately £75,000. The newspaper had at once recognized that a serious wrong had been done, Mr Milmo added, and expressed their willingness to make an unqualified retraction and apology. In addition to meeting the Duchess's costs, they would pay her a substantial sum to underline the gravity of the libel and the sincerity of their apology.

Later that month Margaret was given sixteen days by Lord Wheatley in the Court of Session, Edinburgh, to provide 'better and fuller particulars' of her allegation of adultery between the Duke and her stepmother. The Duke's motion to dismiss her divorce action as irrelevant was refused.

In September, details of George Whigham's will were finally published. As former chairman of British Celanese it was thought that he had substantial assets, but the actual figure for the UK probate was only £226,197 net. With duty paid it was reduced to £219,907. The will made provision for Margaret to receive on trust for herself and her children three-fifths of the balance of the estate after allowing for special gifts. This would provide her with an income of £18,000 a year from the trust, and Brian and Frances £10,000 each. Nothing was provided for his widow. It was said in the High Court that they parted before his death and that a codicil had removed her from among the beneficiaries. To his chauffeur, he left £5,000, a car and a house and to a former housemaid £2,000. There were minor legacies for executors and friends. Jane contested the will, but lost. There was still, however, the separate will concerning Whigham's property in the Bahamas, over which Margaret and Jane fought bitterly for the next fifteen years.

Margaret realized that her father's legacy was far from adequate to allow her to continue her extravagant lifestyle, and sought means to boost her funds – most of which were being eaten up by hefty legal fees from the many writs and petitions she had brought upon herself. Fortunately, she managed to sell the serial rights of her memoirs to the *Sunday People*, which reaped £60,000, a considerable sum for articles that were one-sided in her favour and told little about the real life she led. Litigious as ever, she even tried unsuccessfully to sue her own solicitor, Oscar Beuselinck, a distinguished figure in the legal profession, claiming that he had ill-advised her on the tax liability relating to the earnings from the serial. He rightly pleaded that he had merely, on his client's instructions, negotiated the contract with the newspaper proprietors.

In the summer of that same year, she had lost her claim to the heirlooms she had wanted from Inveraray Castle. Before Lord Wheatley once more, in the Edinburgh Court of Session, it was ruled that her claim to paintings, tapestries and furniture under a Deed of Gift 'was completely invalid'.

Margaret's counsel pleaded that she had alleged that she advanced the Duke £1,000 for five years to enable him to make payments to his former wife in respect of her two children by him. Margaret had also advanced £3,427 to meet the expense of trying to raise the Spanish galleon at Tobermory, and her father advanced substantial sums for the repair and renovation of Inveraray Castle. The Duke in return had executed a Deed of Gift in her favour in 1953. She appealed against the court's decision but lost when Lord Clyde explained that, in 1935, the Duke had entered into a transaction with Equity and Life Assurance in the form of an assignment in order to raise money. He had needed money to marry Louise, and set up their establishment in France, in the expectation of his becoming the next Duke of Argyll. The Duke had undertaken not to give, sell or otherwise dispose of the heirlooms without first obtaining written consent from Equity and Life Assurance. Such consent was never given. 'Clearly,' said Lord Clyde, 'the Duke had no right of property to the heirlooms.' He had been, therefore, in no position to give them to Margaret. 'Upon this ground alone,' Lord Clyde continued, 'the Duchess's case must fail. I am surprised that the Duchess contended she was entitled to disregard the restrictions on the gift and thus be able to sell the family heirlooms stated to be of considerable value, to the highest bidder on the open market.'

It would seem that she had learnt not to pursue costly actions she could not support or hope to win as – either on the advice of her solicitors or her own reasoning – she dropped her divorce action against the Duke in the spring of 1962. Even her lawyers said they did not know that she had dropped the action within minutes of the start of the hearing on 29 May. Jane Whigham was called on to defend her alleged misconduct with the Duke and did not know that the case had been withdrawn when she walked into court with her counsel. The Duke, wearing a light grey lounge suit and striped tie, sat beside Mrs Whigham with whom he had a brief conversation before Margaret's counsel, Mr Walter Fraser, stood in front of Lord Wheatley in the crowded courtroom and said that Margaret was in London and had issued a statement saying that a vital witness had failed to appear at the last moment. 'This witness does not live in the British Isles,' the statement went on, 'and therefore cannot be compelled to attend the Edinburgh Court of Session. There is no doubt, whatsoever, that I shall defend my husband's divorce action against me whenever it is going to be heard.' She added that the abandonment was 'naturally a great disappointment to me and to the people who have helped me'.

Jane recalled that each time she went to London she was shadowed by Margaret's private investigators. Once she received a letter inviting her to join its writer outside the Dorchester where he had a room booked for them both. She informed the police, who advised her to keep the date while they watched. No one appeared, but the police noticed a woman hidden behind a car making notes. A few days later Jane was telephoned by her brother, Leslie Corby, who told her that he had been approached to make a signed statement that his sister and the Duke had committed adultery and that he had been offered £5,000 to make the accusation.

Immediately after Margaret dropped her action to divorce the Duke, Jane instructed her solicitors to start a libel action against Margaret. The writ claimed damages for 'conspiracy to prefer and sustain by illegal means a false and malicious charge of adultery against her, to suborn and bribe a person, or persons, to give false and perjured evidence against her in or for the purpose of legal proceedings based on such charge, to pervert by illegal means the course of justice in such proceedings and to injure her thereby'.

It took another two years for Jane Whigham's case to come to court, but before then, nine months later, Margaret had to undergo the gruelling and embarrassing ordeal of facing Lord Wheatley, the same judge who had already presided over the many actions concerning her, in what went down in legal history as the longest and costliest divorce action in Scottish law. It had taken the Duke four years to prepare his case, and Margaret was faced with the prospect of defending herself against heavy odds.

But then a man came along who was to guide her through the ordeal. He was married, and both he and his wife were Catholic. Margaret began an affair with him in the light of the pending divorce. The Duke had named three men in his petition but he knew nothing of this latest one, who was Margaret's clandestine lover throughout the divorce proceedings and for five years afterwards.

CHAPTER EIGHT

The Divorce Hearing

A LMOST all of 1962 seemed to be taken up by
Margaret's preliminary actions to prevent the Duke
from using her diary in evidence against her in his divorce
petition. The entries about which she was particularly
anxious concerned Peter Combe, one of the men named
in the Duke's petition.

In January, Lord Wheatley said that the Duke sought
divorce from his wife on the grounds of alleged adultery
with three named persons. In the case of one man, the
Duke claimed that a series of meetings, twenty-one in all,
had taken place between July and November 1960. He was
Peter Combe. Lord Wheatley said, however, that entries
in a diary referring to him were the private property of

the writer and entitled to be regarded as confidential. He refused the Duke permission to use the entries as evidence.

Peter Combe, of Strathconan, Muir of Ord, Ross-shire, the son of Lady Moira Combe, who had been one of the great beauties of her day, was given permission by the same court to take evidence from certain witnesses. A week later, Lord Wheatley's decision that the Duke could not use Margaret's diary was reversed by an appeal court and, at the same time, the judges, by a majority of two to one, refused to allow Margaret to amend her defence so as to retract a partial admission about entries in the diary.

However, in April Margaret took her appeal to suppress the information in her diaries to the House of Lords. She wanted to plead that the information was confidential and that the references to Combe should be deleted from the Duke's evidence. But she was refused leave to appeal and told that the proper time to do this would be when the divorce proceedings began in the Edinburgh court.

Mr Walter Fraser, Margaret's barrister, said that she wished to be allowed to amend her evidence relating to a diary kept by her at a time when she was alleged to have been associating with Peter Combe. He referred to the Duke's sworn statement that on 14 July 1960 Margaret had left the 400 Club in Leicester Square accompanied by Combe at 1.30 a.m., and they had gone to her house in Mayfair. There, where they spent an hour and a half together, the Duke alleged that adultery was committed. Mr Fraser said the Duke also alleged that Peter Combe was alone with the Duchess from 4 p.m. to 6 p.m. on 26 October 1960, in her suite at the Ritz Hotel, Paris, and that they then dined together at the Black Diamond.

Margaret argued on each and every minor point of law to the extent of appealing to the Court of Appeal and eventually to the House of Lords on the admissibility of evidence.

A blow to Margaret's confidence occurred two weeks later when, in the High Court of Justice, Mr Justice Plowman continued the hearing of the action by the trustees of the Duke, and Margaret was ordered to deliver up the items the Duke had given her. These included a bronze bust of the ninth Duke on a marble column, six paintings including Roman scenes by Clérisseau, a Zoffany painting valued at £16,000, a harvest scene at Inveraray, five gouache paintings of Swiss landscapes, silver-gilt items, china and a Chippendale-design kneehole desk, valued together at between £22,000 and £25,000.

Finally, on 26 February 1963, almost four years since the Duke had filed his divorce petition, the case opened before the Court of Session in Edinburgh. Lord Wheatley, a Catholic, socialist and Scot – a Campbell on his mother's side – with a sardonic turn of phrase and not lacking in wit, was presiding, before whom Margaret had appeared on so many previous occasions – it must have seemed like old times to both.

The Duke cited three men as Margaret's lovers: Baron Sigismund von Braun, who was now West German Ambassador to the United Nations in New York and was married with five children; John Cohane, fifty-five, an American businessman now living in Ireland; and Peter Combe, former chief press officer at London's Savoy Hotel, now living in Scotland. The Duke's solicitors were Shepherd and Wedderburn, the largest legal firm in Edinburgh. His counsel were George Emslie, QC, and Mr J. H. MacKay. Margaret was represented by Walter Fraser, QC, Dean of the Faculty of Advocates and Head of the Scottish Bar, and Charles Jauncey. Mr A. J. Mackenzie Stuart represented Peter Combe, who denied the Duke's allegations of his adultery with Margaret.

All the public and press seats were filled in the tiny courtroom. The Duke, wearing a grey tweed suit instead of the kilt of the Campbell clan, his normal dress, sat in a second-row seat. Margaret, wearing a light oatmeal-coloured coat, matching hat and a mink wrap, sat in the same row four places away from him.

Equipped with a tightly rolled umbrella and bowler, the Duke's heir, the twenty-five-year-old Marquess of Lorne, sat three seats away from Margaret. They hardly dared look at one another. Lorne and Margaret had been at daggers drawn since she had tried to discredit his paternity. He and his father were staying at the exclusive New Club in Princes Street, patronized by landed Scottish gentry.

The Duke was called as the first witness. After he gave his evidence about the diary, Mr Fraser interrupted to submit that the diary was confidential. The court decided, however, that the diary was allowed as evidence, and Lord Wheatley disallowed the objection.

The Duke gave evidence for five hours on the first day of the hearing. During a week he spent thirteen hours and Margaret twelve in the witness box. One of the witnesses called was Mrs Kathleen Carpenter, personal maid to Margaret for the past twelve years, and later Peter Combe. He was thirty-seven, smartly dressed in a green overcoat with fur collar and cuffs, and wore heavy horn-rimmed glasses.

The case continued for three weeks, but since it was illegal to publish evidence in Scotland there were no verbatim reports of what was said throughout the hearing except those taken by her lawyers.

Margaret, immaculately dressed in a different couture outfit each day of the trial, stayed at the most comfortable hostelry in Edinburgh, the Caledonian Hotel, the best that British Railways could offer. Unknown to anyone, however, she ensconced her lover, a married man with children, in the hotel each weekend. There seemed no end to her resilience – defiance, even – or her determination to do whatever she liked and, true to her nature, she enjoyed the danger involved in this arrangement just as she had so many times before and which was now why she stood before the Edinburgh court.

On 14 March, one Latin word ended the marathon divorce action with an estimated cost of £50,000 in legal fees. At 3.32 p.m. Lord Wheatley spoke the word 'Avizandum', which meant the end of the litigation until his reserved judgment was given, probably two months later, in May.

Margaret was not in court to hear the judgment. She had returned to London, but the Duke was there, with his son to give him moral support. Also present was Peter Combe. There had been nineteen witnesses altogether, twelve for the Duke, five for Margaret and two for Combe. They included experts in forensic medicine and handwriting, private detectives, servants and solicitors. Written evidence was taken from Spain, America and Eire.

Rather than endure the humiliation of listening to the judge's 68,000-word crucifixion in his final summing-up on 8 May 1963 and face the barrage of press reporters and photographers, Margaret had decided to take sanctuary in Paris. The Duke, wearing a grey herringbone suit, his iron-grey hair slicked back, discarded his familiar cigarette holder and sat with his chin cupped in his right hand as he listened to Lord Wheatley's words. He was referred to throughout as 'the pursuer' ('the petitioner' in English courts), and the only co-defendant present, Peter Combe, as 'the party minuter'. The two absent named lovers were called 'the paramours'.

Giving his reserved judgment Lord Wheatley said that Margaret had been promiscuous and her attitude to marriage wholly immoral. He found that the Duke had condoned her adultery with von Braun and the man or men in the photographs.

The judge found, however, that Margaret had committed adultery with Peter Combe, something he was always to deny. He was a bachelor at the time, and he and Margaret were to be seen and photographed frequently visiting theatres and restaurants. Pleasing and attractive, he was also attentive and amusing but she denied having intercourse with him.

Margaret told me this ten years later. She felt that Combe had been done a great injustice in being implicated in her divorce.

Lord Wheatley went on to say that, in effect, four separate cases were embraced in this one action and he considered each in turn. He dealt first with the evidence relating to the three men named and the unnamed man or men in the photographs. He continued with the question of whether these accusations had been established and whether the

Duke had condoned each of them. He dealt finally with the allegation of adultery with Peter Combe, in respect of which no question arose of the Duke having agreed to Margaret's relationship with him.

After a resumé of their marriage from 1951 until 1959 when it broke down, he covered the history of their previous marriages, and the children from the respective unions. He found that the Duke had attributed their unhappiness to Margaret's insatiable desire to participate in social life, while he preferred a quiet existence. Margaret had said that his drinking habits and dislike of any social engagements had much influenced her dependence on the company of others. Lord Wheatley summarized the events just after the Duke's return from the world cruise when he employed a locksmith to open a cupboard in which he found photographs and letters, from von Braun and Cohane, which formed the basis of his case for alleging Margaret's adultery with the two men. The photographs formed his case for alleging adultery with the unnamed man or men.

In referring to the origin of the poison-pen letters, which had confirmed the Duke's resolve to divorce her, Lord Wheatley said that Argyll had found in one of Margaret's cupboards what he considered to be the most important document of all – the mock-up of fragmented documents, pasted on to a piece of notepaper from a hotel, purporting to be a letter written and signed by the Duke's second wife, Mrs Louise Timpson, and the contents of which were highly derogatory of the Duke and his children by the second wife.

The judge said that, in April 1959, the couple had had a violent quarrel and had had no marital relations since, except during one night in June of that year. 'The Duke says that on 12 May 1959 he had a bolt put on his bedroom door to prevent the defender [Margaret] getting into his room and into his bed with him,' the judge continued. 'In cross-examination, the Duke was asked if [Margaret] had admitted to him misconduct with von Braun only to please him, but in her evidence she stoutly denied that she had ever made such an explanation.'

He detailed the events concerning the Duke and his daughter entering Margaret's house and seizing the diary and dwelt at length on this and on the other two diaries which the Duke had taken previously.

'These diaries did not record her innermost thoughts. The general pattern was a record of places she had stayed at, the weather, her engagements and an occasional reference to her health. In the last diary there was an occasional cryptic symbol "B" which the Duke held meant that she had had intercourse with von Braun on that date.

'In support of this, he points out that his own initial appears in her diary for 4 April 1950, when he first had intercourse with her, at that time being married to his second wife. In any event this seems to be somewhat double-edged as there is no "J" on the date on which the Duke alleges that [Margaret] misconducted herself with John Cohane.

'I have reached a decision that the diaries were admissible as evidence. It would be contrary to the interests of justice to prevent a husband, discovering evidence of that nature, from using that evidence against his wife for what it is worth. Further, the use to which these diaries were put in evidence did not in my view constitute unfairness to [Margaret].'

In dealing with the allegations of adultery during 1956, Lord Wheatley said that two were based on letters to Margaret from von Braun and Cohane and the third on photographs. 'The photographs are proved to be photographs of [Margaret] taken during the marriage and they not only establish that she was carrying on an adulterous association with those other men or man but revealed that she was a highly sexed woman who had ceased to be satisfied with normal relations and had started to indulge in what I can only describe as disgusting sexual activities to gratify a basic sexual appetite.'

By today's standards what she was shown doing in the photographs was not extraordinary. The man standing upright, in her bathroom, was naked, his penis erect. She was performing fellatio, crouched on her bended knees, her hand holding his penis. Wrapped round the photographs were sheets of paper captioned 'Before', 'During', 'Oh!' and 'Finished'.

Margaret had, at first, denied that it was her in the photographs but closer examination revealed that one of the fingers of the hand in question bore an Argyll heirloom, a ring that only Margaret had ever worn. Although the head was turned away from the camera – the lens concentrating on the 'subject matter' – the three strands of pearls secured by a diamond clasp round the neck, which had been purchased from Asprey's, were another giveaway. Then, having been forced to admit in court that she was the subject of the photograph, she swore on oath that the penis belonged to none other than her husband. Since the photograph did not show the identifying male face, she felt sure that she was on safe ground by shifting the guilt. But the Duke denied that it was him, and to prove that he was not as well endowed as the man in the photograph he subjected himself to be measured by a doctor. In some ways fortunately, in others not, he proved his case – but he had also to live with the humiliation of publicly declaring his lesser dimensions.

The judge accepted the doctor's opinion, and contended that the photographs depicted Margaret in a position that demonstrated she was engaging in a sexual association with a man who was not her husband, and had been taken, probably, in 1956.

Margaret denied that the photographs indicated adultery. She also denied keeping them, and suggested that they were part of a catalogue of pornographic photographs belonging to her husband. The judge did not accept this theory.

There has been rife speculation throughout the years regarding the identity of the headless man.

The names of several distinguished men have been bandied about over the years and among the favourites were Duncan Sandys, a government minister and son-in-law of Winston Churchill, and Douglas Fairbanks Jnr. The former was dead at the time of the speculation and, therefore, could neither admit nor deny it, while Douglas Fairbanks Jnr categorically refuted the charges on all counts.

Duncan Sandys, however, can be ruled out. During the war, he had stepped on a mine; the operation to mend his wounds left him with scars up the back of his legs and he was slightly disabled from then on. An intimate of Sandys says, 'Apparently, in one of the photographs this "body" was on top of Margaret. There is no way that this could have been Duncan because there were no scars on the back of the legs of the man in the photograph. But I am sure that he *did* have an affair with Margaret all the same. But it wasn't him in the picture.'

Both Sandys and Fairbanks Jnr had won considerable reputations for their manly charms. Moira Lister remembers a close encounter with Sandys, and later, another with Fairbanks Jnr. 'Coming back from a party one night, Duncan said he would give me a lift in a taxi. After we had been in the taxi for about two minutes, he leapt on me, and I started struggling. And then, I thought, Thank God it's a taxi and nobody knows it is me. It's so difficult when somebody's been a dinner guest and suddenly they leap on you. You can't say, "Get off, and leave me alone." So you try to do it politely. In the circumstances. It wasn't too long a drive, and I was able to get away from him. And as I got to my front door, with my key in the latch, the taxi driver called out: "Goodnight, Moira!" I nearly *died*.'

And of Fairbanks Jnr: 'He was very busy with the girls. He tried to jump on me when we made a film at Elstree.'

Fairbanks was idolized by both men and women, and Sir Noël Coward, who had been one of his greatest admirers and closest of friends, summed up the allure in one of his most famous songs, 'Mad About the Boy.'

The photographs had been taken on one of the early Polaroid cameras, first launched in black and white in Boston in 1948. They were not introduced in Britain until 1963. Therefore, anyone in possession of one in 1956 would have brought the camera from the United States. A focus point of two feet to infinity is necessary to take Polaroid pictures, which means that neither subject in Margaret's pictures could have taken them without the use of a self-timer. This technical knowledge would have been essential to the person taking the pictures. The first self-timers for Polaroid cameras were not introduced until the advent of instant colour in 1963 in Britain. But a self-timer for a normal camera could have been used, with technical know-how. As Fairbanks Jnr was a product of the American movie industry he could have been familiar with the latest innovation. But would he have put this new toy to such detrimental use?

Moira Lister says emphatically, and with tact, 'They said it was him. But it wasn't.' And then with conviction, having known the man so well: 'I think the headless man was von Braun.'

If we revert to the judge's summing-up of the divorce case, Lord Wheatley said, referring to a party in New York on 10 January 1956, at which Margaret and Cohane were present, 'Cohane was a self-confessed wolf who admitted he was immediately attracted physically to Margaret and wanted to set in train the machinery culminating in sexual relations.' He added that he could place no reliance on Cohane's evidence once he had departed from the facts. He referred to a series of letters exchanged between Margaret and Cohane, and said that they bore no address or date and were written on scraps of paper from Cohane's office. In the first of these, he had asked Margaret to write to him.

The letters began 'Dearest Margaret' and 'Darling Margaret', indicating that a close personal relationship between them existed: 'You are an incredibly exciting woman' was further proof of the nonsense of Margaret's explanation that there was nothing in their relationship.

"'I am completely frustrated as to how we can get together. I would like to be with you in Paris – what a titillating idea – but I just can't get away,'" the judge read from a passage of one letter. "'I really would love to be with you, even for a few days,'" he read from another, "'and my not having written does not mean that you are not inflaming my imagination. I have thought of a number of new, highly intriguing things that we might do, or I might do to you.'"

'The clear implication,' the judge said, 'was that he had already engaged in a number of "highly intriguing things".' He thought it was conclusive evidence of a previous adulterous association.

"'Darling, I have to leave,'" the judge continued, reading another missive from Cohane to Margaret, "'I miss you enormously, and I never knew that such a short acquaintance could keep a hot flame burning for so long. Much love, Jack.'" Judge Wheatley had no reservations in concluding that Margaret had committed adultery with Cohane on the morning of 13 January 1956.

Turning to the allegations of adultery with von Braun, Lord Wheatley said that he would spare Margaret further embarrassment by not quoting in detail from his letters. He found in the evidence facts, circumstances and qualifications to infer Margaret's adultery with von Braun. 'The position in the present case is that in April 1959, the Duke discovered letters from Cohane and von Braun and the photographs when he had more than a suspicion of her infidelity,' Wheatley continued. 'He was then looking for evidence of her infidelity. But in May 1959, he lived together with the Duchess again and his explanation of this was that he was so shattered at finding the letters that everything else was excluded from his mind for the time being.'

Margaret had contended that the Duke had condoned her relationships, but Lord Wheatley said that he thought the Duke's evidence disputing this was unconvincing. Margaret did not impress him at all: 'Her explanations of many of these incriminating documents were unconvincing and I formed the view that she was lying on various points. She did not shrink from casting aspersions on anyone who seemed to be giving evidence contrary to her interests. She seemed to be a malicious woman.'

The judge continued that there was sufficient evidence to establish that she was a sexually promiscuous woman. 'On her own admission she committed adultery with the Duke before her marriage and with von Braun in the years 1947 to 1950.' She was proved to have committed adultery with Cohane and von Braun: 'She seemed to think association with a married man, or indeed adultery with a married man, was not a serious breach of the moral code if the man was not happy with his wife,' the judge said. 'There is enough in her own admissions to establish that by 1960 she was a completely promiscuous woman whose sexual appetite could only be satisfied by a number of men, and whose attitude to the sanctity of marriage was what moderns would call enlightened, but in plain language could only be described as wholly immoral. These might seem harsh words to use about a woman but she had qualified for them by her own actions, and reference to them was necessary for the proper examination of the law and the administration of justice.'

He referred to the evidence of a man called Peach, a former valet of the Duke who later entered the service of Combe. Lord Wheatley said of Combe: 'My impression of him [Combe] was that he was a liar and a person in whom no trust could be placed.'

The judge concluded that he was convinced that Margaret had committed adultery with Peter Combe, based on evidence in support of this, on the night of 14 July 1960.

He found that the Duke had agreed to her adultery with von Braun and with the unnamed man or men in the photographs, and that he had not agreed her adultery with Cohane. Lord Wheatley granted the Duke a divorce on the grounds of Margaret's misconduct with Combe.

Ten years later, Margaret, seated in her drawing room, said, referring to the outcome of the divorce action, 'The rumours of my diaries swept through London and New York, that I kept these terrible pornographic diaries. I'd kept nothing of the sort. Nothing. And even the judge, God knows he was an old bastard, said they were merely retrogressive reports. All my friends know that at the time of the divorce and for five years afterwards I was involved with someone else. If you want to call it living in sin, then call it living in sin. I think it's the only thing the public haven't read about. But this is a thing that will surprise a lot of people who don't know me well. All my close friends knew, and I'm sure Ian Argyll must have known too, but after 1961 Ian *couldn't* add this man because the judge said this divorce has been added to and fiddled around with long enough, now let's get on with it.

'It was the only genuine thing he *could* have added to the divorce action, but after '61 he had already added poor wretched Peter Combe, who, bless his heart, was charming, and I adored him, but there was no more question of an affair with him than with the man in the moon.'

And then she enlarged on her affair with this mystery lover. His name?

'This is the sixty-four-thousand-dollar question,' she said. 'You see, I can't give his name because he's a married man and his wife kept on threatening suicide all the time.'

However, she had given enough clues and information for me to detect the name of the man she had wanted to marry and to whom she had lost her heart.

CHAPTER NINE

Call It Living in Sin

T HE man with whom Margaret conducted her next
adulterous affair, which lasted over six years from
1961 when she was still married to the Duke, began when
she was embroiled in the divorce action. She encouraged
the liaison in spite of the possible consequences – she
was stimulated by the danger of becoming involved with
the twice-married American, William Hartington Lyons,
referred to by Margaret as Bill. He was the wealthy sales
director of an international American airline company and
lived in Kensington. By the time they met both he and his
Portuguese-born wife, Catusha, were in their late forties,
Catholic and childless. He was dapper, well-mannered,
dark-haired and charming, possessor of all the attributes

Margaret had found attractive in her former lovers. Bill's wife had been brought up by her elder sister after her parents died when she was a baby; he met and fell in love with her in Lisbon where they married in 1954, seven years before he and Margaret became infatuated with one another.

'He isn't English,' Margaret volunteered. 'He took a tremendous risk, because he was in a very big job. And so did I because I was in the middle of the divorce. The press almost got on to it once, but the extraordinary thing was that this was the one time I really *was* in love with somebody and living with him – obviously not in this house. I've never done anything in this house that the servants could raise their eyebrows about. But we were going off on trips all over the world.' She had conveniently forgotten about the pornographic photographs taken in her bathroom and produced in court.

'His father was a lawyer and he was with me right through the divorce. I mean, the ironic thing of it is that Ian, you see,' she tried, nervous of revealing too much information, 'Ian must have had a ghastly time finding evidence against me, because there was nothing to find. He was making up the unknown man and all that – and the photographs, and the diaries.' Whether she was deluded or hallucinating is irrelevant. It is clear that, as a seasoned liar, she was unchanged in her private whitewash campaign.

'But the person he couldn't add was this man, because he'd added too much already, and the judge just couldn't take it. So Ian couldn't add him, but it was the only genuine thing he *could* have. I'm quite sure he knew about him, because we travelled everywhere together. We went on trips all over the world.'

They went to Paris several times, travelling incognito, where, free from the intrusive press and photographers, they were able to conduct their illicit love-affair. Later, after the divorce, in February they made a trip to Cairo on a fifteen-day tour which included a journey up the Nile. They had holidayed together in Sardinia the year before at the time of her appeal against the ruling in the Duke's divorce action. On 27 June 1963, a week after Judge Wheatley granted the Duke his divorce, Margaret attended London's Mayfair Theatre, escorted by Bill Lyons, for a performance of Pirandello's *Six Characters in Search of an Author*. When she went to Anouilh's *Ring Round the Moon* in 1950, the Duke had proposed marriage to her: perhaps she thought that history might repeat itself.

'It was like a marriage. Every time I was asked out to a party, I was asked with *him*. Actually, after Bill left me in 1968, I was awfully crushed for two years, but it *was* a tremendous love-affair. You see, he was as much a third husband to me. The extraordinary thing was that he was up in Edinburgh with me all through the divorce. He wasn't in court, but he came up every weekend. He really was an absolute saint. And he stood by me, and advised me, helped me, prodded the lawyers. He came from a legal family himself, and he'd say, "What the hell are you doing? I don't understand it. Ask them this. Ask them that." I don't know what I would have done without him. And when this ghastly thing was over, there he was. I mean, he was obviously sent from heaven at the moment I needed him. And I would have married him tomorrow, but he had this wife; but I *have* to mention him because otherwise it would look as if I've had a completely sterile life. I would have to take care not to embarrass him. All my *friends* know who it was, but the ordinary public don't.

'It went on for six years, and six years is a long time. And it ended, but he kept coming back, and going away, coming back and going away, until it drove me up the wall. I mean, he didn't have the courage to, you know, "get out". He didn't have moral courage at all like the average man does. It's an extraordinary story because he was a Leo and he was a typical Leo. And a Leo always defends the underdog. And nobody was more the underdog than I was. And he defended me almost with a sword. I mean, if that was the time of swords, he would have a sword out. And of course this is very Leo, isn't it? He wasn't arrogant, but he was tremendously possessive. Possessive to a point of mania, the way my first husband was. I simply engender this possessiveness in people, and I don't know why, because really, I'm the faithful type.

'He went back to his wife because she kept on threatening suicide, suicide,' she repeated the word involuntarily because of her stammer, 'all the time. And all I needed was that, to live on a clifftop all the time. It was an awful heartbreak for me when it broke up. I don't think I've been through anything like it in my life. I've never *been* so miserable.'

Perhaps Margaret was told by her lovers that their wives had threatened suicide if they deserted them, but it is unlikely. It is what she wanted to hear them say. For these men, their wives were a safety net. No man in his right mind would have forsaken his wife, his children, his career and his home for Margaret. She was already fifty and with something of a reputation. Also Bill's wife was a staunch Catholic and therefore neither suicide nor divorce would have entered her head.

Margaret was clearly deluded; even deluded enough to believe that the Duke loved her romantically. Perhaps she mistook sex for love.

'I don't think that Ian ever loved anybody the way he loved me. I will say that. I think he adored me. A sort of love–hate thing. I don't know what happened. I really don't. I still don't know to this day what happened, because I tried very hard. There was that period of building up this divine place and being his wife, being at the head with the Chief, as a star. I loved it. And then came the period of traumatic horror. That was from 1960 till, well, it's gone on pretty well for ten years. I mean the divorce was the climax, but it went on being revived. It was revived with the Denning Report. It was revived with Ian's newspaper articles. I went through that divorce about three times, publicly.

'Then after the divorce came a period of tremendous travel. I travelled the world with Bill and adored it. I did a great deal of travelling with him. And that was also a tremendous escape. I don't like the word escape, because I wasn't really escaping anything. I sat here and faced it. God knows, I faced it. Some people find escape playing the violin, and some people find it doing the crossword puzzles. But I find travelling is a tremendous therapy. Just getting to an airport – all the rest fades away. Getting into the aeroplane, and knowing it's going to Dakar, or somewhere. Then I begin to concentrate on that, and forget the other horrors. And then I come back to face the horrors again.

'When I used to come back, I used to wonder what was going to hit me. What long brown envelope, what writ would arrive. Because it becomes a pattern. You can sue and get money out of her. This is what happened. They say, "She's lost one case, a thousand pounds, we'll get it on the same." And so I used to wonder who would writ me next. And what ghastly people would approach me.'

The affair with Bill Lyons could not have lasted for two reasons. Margaret enjoyed the trappings of being a duchess and although the Duke remarried shortly after their divorce, she was still entitled to the courtesy and dignity afforded her while she carried the title, Margaret, Duchess of Argyll. She would never have accepted being a plain Mrs, no matter how much she loved the man.

'Our affair ended in sixty-eight,' Margaret said regretfully. 'No, it didn't just peter out. He wouldn't come near me now, because he knows if he did, it would just start all over again.

'When Bill came into my life it was heaven. What I went through with Ian publicly was ghastly. Ghastly, ghastly, ghastly. Nothing on earth could have been more dreadful to live through. But it wasn't only because he was a duke and I was duchess, because I had been this great star without any scandal until I married him. All of a sudden I fell from the greatest heights down to the ground with a crash. That is what made it so interesting from the public point of view. I have been in the news for a long time. Wherever I go, and I couldn't be more embarrassed having to keep on saying this, wherever I go all over the world there are articles about me. Leading articles, which aren't about the divorce.

'I am news just because it's *me*. This is without Ian, without the Duke, without a husband. You see, Nicole [the

Duchess of Bedford] was made by Ian Bedford, the Duke.
Diana Napier's name was *made* by Richard Tauber. And
I put Ian Argyll on the map. Nobody had ever *heard* of
Ian before. He was a Campbell up to the age of forty-nine,
and I put him on the map. My father and I poured a lot
of money into Inveraray Castle, but we never said a word
about it, because Ian was very difficult.

'You've got to keep a man's ego and pride, besides, it's
not an attractive thing to talk about. Ian hadn't a *bean*.
Careless, all right. Nobody cares, but when people use
this awful term about me, "Deb of the Year", it makes me
climb up the wall because I was more than just that. After
all, when I married Charlie Sweeny, I married, in a way, a
commoner, who was a very glamorous man but he had no
great wealth, or title or anything. I made *him*. I put *him* on
the map. And as a couple we were tremendously glamorous.
If Charlie had married a Miss Jones you would never have
heard of him again.'

Of course Bill Lyons remained in the shadows. He did
not want publicity.

'Bill and I travelled all over the world, but I didn't want
to go to my father's house in Nassau. I've never liked resorts.
I hate Deauville, I hate Monte Carlo, I hate Palm Beach. You
name them. I hate them. When I'm travelling I only like
staying with friends when I'm awfully free to do what I want.
And if I'm in an unknown place, like a jungle, obviously it's

nicer to stay in a house with people who show you around. If I'm in a very big city like Paris, or Rome or New York, I'd rather be in a hotel. For instance, I was going to stay with Mary Martin in Brasília, but then her husband Richard Halliday died. That's the kind of place you *must* stay with somebody. You can't go live in the jungle on the top of a tree. I mean, happiness comes in a lot of ways, doesn't it?'

Moira Lister said, 'Bill Lyons was a very nice man. He was very unprepossessing, but he wasn't in the same league as von Braun. But he was a very, very nice executive-type man who didn't have much to say for himself but I think she hung on to him because he was a very real person. He wasn't one of the blades about town. I don't remember him saying very much or having much sense of humour or being very bright. But he was very solid. A nice, good-looking man, and I think that probably because he was different from the others he gave her a sort of solidity, which she was looking for, without having to settle for it totally. He was a very good friend.

'I don't know about the lover side of it. But he was very much in attendance, but never much part of the scene. He was sort of there, but not there. He never joined into the party spirit but stood aside. He was very attentive, very sweet, awfully nice, but colourless. Perhaps that is what she liked, a man who wouldn't steal her limelight. He worked for Pan American Airways.'

Although Margaret was never renowned for her wit, when she broke up with Bill, she announced, 'From now on I travel TWA.'

She picked up the thread of the story: 'I haven't seen Bill for six years, but if he wanted to, I'd marry him tomorrow. *Tomorrow*. I love being married. I miss talking to somebody, finding out what they're doing. I have to admit I miss Ian. I was a tremendous friend to Ian Argyll. That's what I like too, to be behind a man. To push him. To help him. Of course I'd love to be with somebody.'

But because of her background and financial independence she was certain that she frightened many men away. 'I think more money and independence make for more difficulty in the relationship. I think I'm something rather strange that men can't understand. I want to be protected very much, but one can't wait for ever for that glorious man to come round. I think that living alone is an art and you have to make the most of it. An awful lot of women, married women who are alone, try it but can't do it. You can't sit around in a kind of sewing circle waiting for the telephone to ring, then having women-only luncheons. If you're alone you've got to get out and make your life. Make it an interesting and amusing life. But get the hell out of the house. I have no anxiety about telephoning somebody to say, "Look, I've got two theatre seats. Are you free?" I'd do it tomorrow. Lots of women find it difficult going into restaurants and signing or paying the bill but although I wouldn't have to go out because I've got this house and entertain at home, if I had to give dinner to six people in a restaurant I'd sign the bill and that wouldn't worry me. But if I'm with a man alone, I'd say to the place I'm going to in advance, "Don't produce a bill. Send it to me.'"

She relied on the fact that Bill's father was a lawyer, when, in 1960, she entered into an agreement with News International to publish her memoirs in the *Sunday Pictorial* with every expectation of winning the divorce action. No question of legal costs, large or small, came into the contract and she asked the distinguished lawyer Oscar Beuselinck to her house to seek his advice. Bill was present on that occasion when the two of them discussed matters concerning the exploitation of her life and personality.

Seven years later, in an action that was to take five years before final judgment in the High Court, she unsuccessfully sued Beuselinck, father of the dashing British singer and actor Paul Nicholas, over tax matters regarding the income from the memoirs.

She claimed that after tax she had received only £20,000 profit from the £55,000 fee from the articles. It was a considerable sum in those days to be paid by a newspaper for a 'kiss-and-tell' serialization. Mr Beuselinck naturally defended the action and issued a summons to strike out her claim.

In her sworn affidavit she sought recovery of tax and her costs. Explaining that agent's commission reduced the £55,000 to £38,000 of her very considerable income, she bore a high rate of taxation which made her liability £34,000. She contended that if the agreement had been for the sale of her diaries, papers, photograph albums and so on, this would have ranked as sale of materials and been untaxable. She suggested that of the £55,000 a total of £53,000 should have been expressed to have been in respect of 'materials'.

She claimed that Oscar Beuselinck never asked her whether she would sell her diaries, but the judge, Mr Justice Megarry, said that he preferred Mr Beuselinck's recollection that he did ask her, but that she refused.

In giving his reserved judgment, the judge added, 'I think that the defendant [Mr Beuselinck] was brought in primarily in respect of defamation, and that he introduced the subject of copyright and emphasized the importance of retaining copyright for the purposes of the proposed multiple ventures.

'Mr Lyons, a friend of the plaintiff [Margaret], had made previous inquiries of other solicitors as to Mr Beuselinck's suitability for this type of work.'

When the action was finally resolved in the High Court she lost the case and was ordered to pay the costs which were expected to exceed the £13,940 she had claimed.

The judge concluded, 'I hold that the defendant [Mr Beuselinck] was not guilty of negligence towards the plaintiff [Margaret]. It follows that this claim fails and must be dismissed.'

And so it was.

Over twenty years later, Oscar Beuselinck told the author, 'There was very little factual disagreement at the time. And now, with hindsight, and at a greater age, I feel that she was being very silly about it all.'

When her memoirs were published, Lord Francis-Williams aired his views about her divorce in a derogatory piece in the *New Statesman*, and Lord Hailsham chose the sanctuary of the House of Lords to profess indignation that her articles were an affront to a 'Christian country'.

It was not in her nature to take criticism lying down. She chose the platform of the *Sunday Mirror* on 23 June 1963 to vent her spleen, attacking their lordships for being so outspoken about her adulterous marriage to the Duke. She, herself, had already done so in the articles.

After Lord Francis-Williams and Lord Hailsham had had their say, the following month Lord Denning himself entered into the fray when he sent for the record of the Argyll divorce case in his inquiry into the Profumo scandal. He had taken an intense interest in widespread gossip about certain aspects of the divorce and called for the papers to be sent up to London from Scotland.

Lord Denning had interviewed Dr Stephen Ward and four other people twenty-four hours earlier regarding the John Profumo affair when Christine Keeler was found to be having a simultaneous affair with Profumo, Minister of Defence, and Eugene Ivanov, military attaché to the Russian Embassy. It was said that he was led into the field of inquiry by Mr Harold Macmillan's declaration in setting up the investigation, that rumours were circulating which affected the honour and integrity of public life in Great Britain and which, if they were true, could indicate a grave security risk. Margaret's high government contacts and her friendship with Anthony Eden and Duncan Sandys made her a possible security risk.

Having agreed to be interviewed by Lord Denning for the preparation of the famous 'Denning Report', Margaret stipulated that she would only talk to him on the understanding that the discussion would be confidential.

She was remarkably ill prepared for news of a more domestic nature the next month, August. Although she had been enjoying her affair with Bill Lyons in the months leading up to her divorce from the Duke, no one could have been more surprised than she when she discovered that the Duke had, at the same time, been conducting a clandestine relationship with another woman. Her first knowledge of their liaison came when she read reports in the press of the Duke's marriage three weeks after their acrimonious divorce became final. Her own wedding had taken place a mere three hours after the Duke's divorce from Louise, so she could not have been entirely surprised at the speed and methods employed by the mercurial Argyll. The ceremony took place two days before his sixtieth birthday, his fourth marriage, at Horsham, Sussex, on 15 June 1963. The union was sealed with every intention of him and his new wife producing the child Margaret had failed to provide, with or without his aid. The object of his *amour* was an American, Mrs Mathilda Coster Mortimer, who had lived in Paris for several years. She was in her late thirties and had three sons from her marriage to Professor Clemens Heller, a lecturer at the Paris University. After their divorce in 1961, ironically the year in which Margaret had begun her six-year affair with Bill Lyons, Mathilda reverted to her maiden name. 'I've lived most of my life in cities,' Mathilda explained soon after the marriage. 'Then, since my parents were American, I was sent to stay with a grandmother in New York during the war. I got a degree in philosophy at the girls' college of Harvard, and after the war I returned to Paris and got married.'

After her divorce she went to live in Scotland where she stayed with friends in Strachur, a village twenty-five miles from Inveraray Castle, and since the Duke's family and hers were old friends they got to know each other better during the next two years.

By the end of the year, Mathilda announced that she was expecting the Duke's child but, by the end of March the following year, she had had a miscarriage. She lost a second baby the next year, too. In 1968 she gave birth to a baby prematurely, weighing only 2 pounds 12 ounces, who died shortly after birth at the Royal Maternity Hospital, Glasgow.

If Margaret had felt that her past was behind her, at any rate with regard to her ten-year marriage to the Duke, she was mistaken. She was haunted and persecuted by further legal actions, one following the other. She had brought them all on herself.

When Margaret's stepmother issued a writ against her in June 1962 for libel, Margaret could not have known that it would take over two years for the action to come to court in October 1964. Jane Whigham issued a writ against Margaret and Mrs Gail Corby for damages, 'for conspiracy to prefer and sustain by illegal means a false and malicious charge of adultery against her'.

On 26 October 1964 Mr Justice Hinchcliffe in the High Court approved a settlement by Margaret to pay £25,000 libel damages to Jane Whigham, plus costs. It was announced in open court after counsel representing the parties had seen the judge privately in his room. Although Margaret was not in court, Jane Whigham was present to hear the court's decision in her favour. In the out-of-court settlement, Mr Geoffrey Crispin, QC, for Jane, told the judge that agreed terms of settlement had been drawn up. Margaret had, once more, thrown in the towel at the bitter end.

It was agreed that Jane Whigham's claims of conspiracy, malicious prosecution and injurious falsehood were to be dismissed, and Margaret had agreed to pay up in respect of the libels complained of. The judge added that 'All parties are undertaking that, so as to avoid any further publicity about this dispute, none of them will make any statement or comment hereafter about it to anyone.'

'I was horrified to be accused of such an act,' the Duke said, when Jane Whigham won her five-year battle with Margaret, who had named him as co-respondent. 'It was probably the most dreadful of all the monstrous allegations with which I have had to contend.' It was impossible for him to sue Margaret since her allegation was made while he was still married to her. But he regarded the payment of the damages as a vindication of himself as well as of Mrs Whigham. Such a 'monstrous allegation' was not in fact so far from the truth as the Duke had suggested. Jane Whigham was later to admit that she had indeed conducted an affair with the Duke, but only after the divorce.

Undaunted by this setback, Margaret took legal action once again when she applied to the Chancery Court judge to prevent the Duke from publishing his life story in the *People* newspaper, including the publication of private letters between himself and the Duchess. These intimacies, she claimed, were communicated to him in confidence during their marriage, and 'not hitherto made public property'.

In the first of his articles, one of the Duke's complaints about Margaret was that she had become haughty when in public with him, always seeking the limelight and press attention. Once when he had been dining with Margaret at one of his favourite restaurants, Maxim's, in Paris, he discussed the menu with the head waiter, Albert. He had also asked the man about his family and general well-being. Margaret had felt she was left out of the conversation and resented the Duke's familiarity with 'small people', as she generally referred to waiters, staff and shop assistants. She retired to the powder room where she sulked for over an hour, leaving the Duke to eat his meal alone. Hers remained untouched. She returned to the table after he had settled the bill, and then, still in a huff like a spoiled child, asked to be taken home. It was her way of punishing him for ignoring her while he 'held court' with a member of the distinguished restaurant's staff.

On other occasions, at Inveraray Castle, when the newspapers were brought up to their bedroom in the morning she became upset when she found that her name was not mentioned in the social or gossip columns. If there happened to be an unfavourable comment about her, she would fly into a rage, pummelling him on the head when he was barely awake, fuming, 'Ian! Read this. See what they're saying about me. Wake up. Come on, wake up! You've got to stop them. Telephone the editor at once. Get a retraction. An apology. Sue. Sue them. You've got to sue them. You can't let them say these horrible things about me!'

In her affidavit at the hearing in November 1964 after publication of the first article, Margaret claimed that by 1956, five years after the marriage, the Duke had begun to treat her with vindictive hostility. She had lost respect for him and the marriage ended in disaster. She believed that the Duke had continued to pursue her with implacable enmity and would stop at nothing to damage her reputation if he possibly could. She claimed that for a number of years before the marriage began to deteriorate they had a close and intimate relationship. They had freely discussed matters of a strictly private nature, including their past lives, previous marriages, business and private affairs – intimacies they would not have divulged to anyone else. She said it would be painful and embarrassing for her if the Duke were to reveal the intimate details of their married life. Her stepmother, a year younger than herself, she stressed, had regarded her with a venomous hatred, comparable to that of the Duke.

She had, of course, forgotten that she had done precisely the same thing when she sold her own memoirs, which largely concerned their married life, for £55,000 without the Duke bringing pressure to bear on her.

In his own affidavit, the Duke said he had begun to suspect that Margaret had committed adultery by 1956 and from then his feelings naturally became cooler: 'By reason of her conduct in that and other ways I have lost all respect and affection towards her,' and claimed that he had never made any disclosure in breach of any trust or confidence arising out of their marriage and did not intend doing so. However, he found it necessary to reveal her discreditable conduct in the interests of justice and to preserve the honour of his family name and himself. He scoffed at the idea that Margaret had found publicity unwelcome. He criticized the articles she had written for the press, suggesting that they were designed to create a favourable public image for herself and to show him as the villain of the piece. They had created a false impression which he felt it necessary to correct.

Sir Andrew Clark, acting for Margaret, said that the Duke's third article, due to appear the next day, was by far the most objectionable in the series. It had been rewritten but it was no better than before. Among other things, it contained what purported to be a verbatim report of a doctor on Margaret's physical health and condition in the early days of the marriage. 'How any man with any decent feelings could seek to publish such a thing to the world for his pecuniary benefit passes comprehension.'

Perhaps, in a form of retribution for having been forced to pay such a substantial sum to Jane Whigham for the harm she had done to her character and reputation, notwithstanding the inexcusable accusation of adultery she had inflicted on the Duke, Margaret hoped to gag both the press and the Duke with regard to his forthcoming *exposés* destined for the *People* newspaper.

The legal bantering between Margaret and the Duke had gone on for years. They vied with one another, both showing cast-iron determination to have their own way. In some senses they both lost, but the Duke had, at least, won his freedom from her.

The court ruled in her favour, defining the principle of privileged communication between spouses and others. 'It also protects writers who can show that they have copyright in their material.' But in all other respects it upheld that freedom of speech (which includes the freedom to repeat what others say) was thought to be unfettered, subject to the general laws of libel and obscenity.

The judge drew on that precedent to uphold the arguments for Margaret. He said that because marriage was a contract and a relationship of mutual trust in which the secrets of private life were exchanged, Margaret was entitled to claim the court's protection against the Duke.

After the hearing the Duke said, 'It is a matter of regret to me that a judge has forbidden me to make certain disclosures concerning events that occurred during my former marriage. I felt it was necessary that I should give my answer to the statements she made, and especially so because I was then a party to a series of lawsuits involving my wife, a wealthy woman, and I was called upon to find a substantial sum of money to meet my legal costs. I saw no reason why the public should still not be given my side of the story which, if I had been allowed to tell it in full, would, I believe, have disposed of the rumours and false allegations that are still in circulation.'

On returning to his club, White's, the Duke was informed that he had been expelled. Gentlemen do not tell tales on their wives, even if their wives had behaved unconventionally.

Although it had been proved without any possible doubt that he had been the injured party in the marriage, Margaret had managed to shift the guilt so that she could appear as the damsel in distress.

However, the Duke seemed to be shot of Margaret and her gripes once and for all. He had remarried and seemed happy with his new wife and lifestyle.

Margaret was still enjoying her love-affair with Bill Lyons but the relationship she had with her children was far from easy. Brian and Frances seemed far away from her thoughts – on the other hand she had never been close to them – and on her return from Egypt, and with the many court cases behind her, she realized that she had lost a great many friends and some of her considerable social standing. She felt it was time to attend to the welfare of her grandchildren and try, at least, to spend time with them. But she was in for a bitter shock. Frances, embarrassed by the publicity her mother attracted, decided to cut herself and her children off from Margaret.

And Brian was involved in a serious road accident in New York in which he was almost crushed to death.

CHAPTER TEN

Friends, Family and Foes

WHEN the sex revolution came to London, in the early 1960s with Beatlemania, Carnaby Street and the youth cult, Margaret looked on it all as *passé*. She had done and seen it all. Her own moral standards had dissipated far further and rather before those of the young during the so-called swinging sixties. On the one hand, the girl-next-door look, exemplified by Twiggy, was headline news, but on the other, the way-out freaky look with weird and exotic models, showing clothes no one could wear, became the 'in thing'. Nostalgia began to creep in under the Biba label, but, in contrast, astronauts inspired

Courrèges and Cardin with space-age cuts. Mary Quant was responsible for slashing skirts to such new heights that the miniskirt was born.

While a new generation of photographers, David Bailey, Norman Eales, Brian Duffy, Terence Donovan and Barry Lategan, rivalled America's Richard Avedon, Irving Penn, Melvin Sokolsky and Britain's Norman Parkinson, Margaret remained safely with her own interpreters, Dorothy Wilding and Brodrick Haldane.

For traditionalists such as Margaret, the changes were hard to accept. Although she smoked cigarettes, and drank the occasional glass of white wine over dinner, she never took drugs. She also refused to be swayed by the new fashions, and, wisely, kept to her own individual style. She always wore low-key, unostentatious clothes, beautifully cut, made by the top *haute couture* houses in London and Paris, and never changed her style of make-up. It evoked her 1930s heyday, with pale complexion and bright red lipstick. Her matching nail varnish was never chipped or cracked.

By the time she reached fifty, her hair was beginning to thin a little and she relied on a small, undetectable hairpiece to pad out what remained. She was helped to change her 1930s image when Moira Lister's husband, Jacques, the Vicomte d'Orthez, told her: 'You've got this beautiful face, Margaret. But your hairstyle is out of date. You must take it all up and make it look modern.'

'And from that date,' Moira Lister said, 'she kept the new hairstyle and it suited her. She had a tiny hairpiece on the top, and she kept that style and handled it right until the day she died, and she always looked absolutely wonderful. And that skin, of course,' she continued. 'It had never seen the sun. That is the prime example when beauticians say you should never go near the sun. She never, ever, saw a peek of sun on her skin with the result that she looked fantastic. She looked absolutely wonderful.'

Film stars always look like film stars. They did in those days, at any rate. Garbo, Dietrich, Joan Crawford, Vivien Leigh and the other great movie actresses never changed the image for which they became immediately identified, both in features and in dress. Margaret had learnt from them and always kept her own recognizable persona intact. She considered herself a star and maintained the lifestyle of one.

But she remained the star of the law courts and the popular press rather than of the stage or screen.

Moira Lister, who has innate star quality, added, 'She really should have been an actress without having to create all those incidents in order to *get* the limelight. She could have been a silent star. She clamoured for attention. She needed attention because she was a great, great beauty and felt that she had something to give, and *demanded* attention. And she was quite right, because she was a ravishing lady. But when she commanded attention she didn't do so by falling down drunk, or lifting her skirts up or making an idiot of herself. She was always dignified. But all the things the press got hold of was her life behind doors. It was *her* life and they got hold of it. But, of course, she invited them to get hold of it. She needed a stage, really. That is her epitaph.'

Although Margaret's daughter, Frances, was like her in many ways, she wanted none of the press attention or glory her mother craved. She certainly did not want to be involved in any way despite her mother implicating her in the poison-pen letter scandal. Moreover, she gave the Edinburgh Court a wide berth throughout Margaret's divorce action.

The Duchess of Rutland and her husband were very private people. Frances resented her mother's lifestyle, her notoriety and her betrayal of the Catholic faith. How could she possibly be a product of such a mother?

There has been speculation throughout the years about the estrangement between the two duchesses.

'Isn't that always the way with children of famous parents?' Moira Lister continued. 'The children come along and say, "I don't want to be the way my mother was, or the way my father was." And they rebel against that. And I think that's why Frances remained very Catholic and very apart because she didn't want to compete with her mother.'

Moira Lister, a devout Catholic herself, believes that the reason for the enmity between Frances and her mother went back many years. 'It stemmed from the time when Margaret took Frances and the Duke of Rutland to the Pope to get an annulment of Charles's [Rutland] marriage. She was desperate for Frances to marry him so that Frances could become a duchess. There seems to have been a falling out from that time. The reason she took Frances and Charles to the Pope was because Charles had been married before, he had a daughter by his first marriage and he was Church of England. So they couldn't marry in a Catholic church and get a full Catholic wedding. She tried for an annulment and because she wasn't able to achieve it they weren't able to get married in a Catholic church. I think that was the start of the rift, so that when the children came they would have to be brought up in the Catholic faith. If Charles was going to marry her it would have to be on condition that the children would be brought up Catholic, which they were. Once a Catholic, always a Catholic, until you are excommunicated, so that if you choose to go to another faith, you are excommunicated because you are no longer in the Roman Catholic faith.'

Frances had no intention of changing her faith and because the Duke of Rutland had no desire to change his, much as Margaret would have favoured a large wedding, similar to her own in the Brompton Oratory, the couple married at Caxton Hall.

David, Marquess of Granby, was born on 8 May 1959 and suffered from part paralysis of the right side. Moira Lister particularly remembers their daughter, Theresa. 'She was a most beautiful girl. She was at school with my daughter Christabel at St Mary's, Ascot. Her mother, Frances, is the godmother to Christabel.'

Some years later, Lady Theresa Manners joined a rock band in which she was lead singer. Or, at any rate, made a pretty good stab at it. Moira Lister recalls being invited with her husband to attend one of Theresa's performances at the London Hippodrome, as guests of Frances and Charles Rutland: 'I remember, it was quite appalling. She couldn't sing. She was gyrating and doing all that kind of stuff, and Frances's face was a picture of absolute horror. Charles was quite amused about it, saying "Well, I suppose they go through this phase, don't they?" She was a beautiful child, but she couldn't sing. And then she gave it up and went to New York where she wanted to be an actress but that didn't work either. She wasn't cut out for it. Apparently she's got over all that now. I daresay it was her one sort of outlet.'

However, Margaret was happy about the arrangement. When sitting on Moira's balcony in Belgravia, she said, 'At least my granddaughter is following in my footsteps. She wants to be a star. Like me. I think it's rather good she's gone and done all that. Coming out of a convent and letting loose that way.'

The rock band finally disintegrated, and Lady Theresa gave up the stage for good.

The Rutlands' second child, Robert, died aged two and a half of leukaemia but in 1965 Frances gave birth to another boy, whom they named Edward and who later became a high-powered executive for British Airways.

Much as Margaret wanted to play the role of doting Granny, she was prevented from so doing by her daughter. And that same year Margaret, herself, was threatened with a death in the family.

That of her own son, Brian.

The year had begun happily enough when she and Bill toured Peru, Patagonia and Mexico for six weeks and, after their return to London, then spent a few days in Paris. Memories of the time she had spent at the Ritz with the Duke were still too vivid for Margaret to contemplate taking her new lover there. For Bill's sake, and also for fear of being seen by the staff of the Ritz, who knew her well and might comment on her being accompanied by a married escort, she chose another fashionable luxury hotel, the Plaza Athenée.

While lunching with friends, the Baron and Baronne de Cabrol, in their Avenue Foch apartment during that visit, Margaret received a telephone call from Charles Sweeny in

London. He had been given her number by the concierge at the Plaza Athenée, whom she had told of her luncheon arrangements. Sweeny told her that their son Brian had been involved in a car accident in New York. Apparently his Porsche had been flattened by a pantechnicon crossing 84th Street. He had been rushed to the Lennox Hill Hospital where he was under observation in the intensive care unit. Almost every bone down the right-hand side of his body was broken.

Margaret arranged to set off for New York immediately, stopping *en route* in London to summon her maid to pack her bags. Before she left for New York, she discovered that her stepmother, Jane Whigham, had remarried, aged forty-nine. She and her second husband, Wing Commander Clive Beadon, spent their honeymoon in the Whigham house, Seahaven, on the north shore of Nassau. Margaret resented the intrusion, but the property remained the subject of litigation, until her father's will and Jane's claim under a Bahamas 'dower right' to the property were proved valid. Margaret knew that she would have to give in over the ownership of the estate, but until the matter was resolved the lawyers had agreed mutually that both women had the right of occupation under the terms of the trust. Separately.

'The property has been let,' Margaret said ten years later. 'The battle has been going on for fourteen years with my stepmother, and I've got to give in. It's really cost me money to fight her. So much. Besides, I don't like it there. I'm trying to get rid of it. I'm selling it,' she added, although she had no legal right so to do.

She discovered, too, that Louise Timpson had secretly divorced her third husband, the New York investment banker Robert Timpson, the year before. 'It was all kept very quiet,' Louise said. 'I divorced my husband last June on the grounds of incompatibility. It had nothing to do with his expulsion from the Stock Exchange.' It appeared that Timpson's securities firm had gone into liquidation in 1962, and at the beginning of 1963 he was expelled by the New York Stock Exchange. He went to start a new life in South Africa. 'My elder son [the Marquess of Lorne] spent Christmas with me and my younger son, Lord Colin Campbell, is farming at Tequite near Wellington, New Zealand. I am very proud of both my sons.'

Louise Timpson died seven years later at her home at Rhinebeck, New York, aged sixty-four.

Margaret stayed in New York for several months, ostensibly to be at her son's bedside. She knew that Frances was expecting another baby and that she would be welcome neither at its birth nor for the christening. She prolonged her stay in New York to save face and to prevent family friction. Had she been in Britain for the birth and found by friends and press alike to have been banned from Belvoir, she would have had no ready excuse. To stay in the shadows was one of the wisest decisions she had been made to make.

Ever on the move, and with Bill as head sales executive of the American airline company to make her travel arrangements, Margaret flew to Rome in June that year. She spent the weekend there to attend the wedding of Princess Olimpia Torlonia, granddaughter of ex-Queen Ena of Spain. She married the twenty-five-year-old Paul-Annik Weiller, son of a French industrialist, whose mother had married Sir John Russell, British ambassador to Ethiopia, Brazil and Spain, and later Chairman of Rolls-Royce.

By October, Margaret had become restless again. Aware that her name had not appeared in the newspapers for some months because of her extensive travels abroad, she stirred up a bizarre story for the popular press. She contacted Scotland Yard to complain that she had received a number of telephone calls and letters with threats to kill her. A string of her enemies would have willingly carried out the deed without hesitation, but none was sufficiently courageous to do so. Margaret felt obliged to fabricate the incidents.

The police checked callers to the house the night before, put a twenty-four-hour guard on her Mayfair house, intercepted telephone calls and fingerprinted the death-threat letters, but largely with tongue in cheek. They had been through it all before. And they would go through the ritual again on the next occasion she complained that jewels worth £20,000 had been stolen from her collection. They turned up three days later by which time she had achieved the much desired press coverage for her publicity campaign.

After several operations, and almost eight months since the car accident, Brian returned to England where he spent a few days convalescing with Frances at Belvoir Castle. 'I am still on crutches,' he said while he was there, 'but I have a series of exercises to do, and I hope that within about six weeks I shall be able to walk normally. I plan to stay with my mother until the New Year and then go for a holiday to Jamaica. And after that I shall go back to work in New York,' which, indeed, he did. But within three years the stockbroking company for which he worked went into liquidation and he returned to London where he entered a new career with an investment company. By the time he reached his mid-fifties, Brian was divorced and had a son and daughter.

While he was staying with Frances he saw the new baby, the fourth child born to the Rutlands. Lord Edward Manners had arrived on 29 May when Brian was still in hospital in New York. 'Edward was absolutely beautiful,' Moira Lister enthused. 'He was a gorgeous-looking child.'

Frances continued to resist all attempts at her mother contacting her children. Despite Moira Lister's explanation about the enmity between Margaret and Frances stemming from Margaret's failure to persuade the Pope to annul the Duke of Rutland's first marriage, the reason was far more deeply rooted. She could never forgive her mother for having implicated her in the poison-pen letter scandal six years before. It was inconceivable for her to accept that her own mother could behave in such a callous manner without regard to the consequences for her children or her stepchildren. Frances had suffered the indignity of being brought before the judge at the Scottish Court to give evidence against her mother. It seemed almost as much as she could bear. Frances was afraid that her mother's notoriety might somehow harm her children and wanted to protect them from her. Margaret's powerful presence could threaten the structure of their respectable family life. The sanctity of her family was of paramount importance to her and her children. Public conflict never erupted between mother and daughter. Frances has been careful throughout the years not to bring any element of disharmony or friction to the Rutland name or to her family's future. Her eldest son became the next Duke of Rutland and she wisely safeguarded his heritage. Sadly, Margaret had not given her own daughter such consideration when she implicated her in the scandal. The estrangement meant that Margaret would never see her grandchildren grow up, though she followed their lives through the press and kept photographs.

Having been put firmly in her place by her daughter and without legal entanglements to occupy her time, Margaret decided to accept an invitation to go to Mexico in February 1966. She flew to Los Angeles for the start of her three-month sojourn. While she was there she met the immensely rich Baron and Baroness di Portanova from Houston, Texas. The half-Neapolitan Ricky's Texan grandfather had been one of the richest men in Houston, and his wife, the dark-haired Yugoslav-born Ljuba, had film-star looks and a collection of jewels that she wore on every possible occasion at her husband's behest. She could have rivalled the Queen of Sheba. They became lifelong friends of Margaret's and always entertained her when they stayed in their suite at Claridge's in London.

Ricky di Portanova had the looks and the charm of Clark Gable and was an extremely generous man. He was a well-known frequenter of the most exclusive casinos in the world and was popular wherever he and Luba went. Many years later, in the mid-seventies on one of their visits to London, Margaret was feeling particularly desperate for male company. Ricky did not want to get involved.

'Ricky,' Margaret said to him, 'sometimes I feel I need a man so desperately that my body aches. Is there anyone you know?' She hoped that in his immense circle of friends there would be men who might come to her assistance.

She went first to Los Angeles where she dined with George Getty, her old friend Paul's son, then followed her itinerary to Mexico City, where in Cuernavaca she visited Merle Oberon, then married to Bruno Pagliai, and went on to Guatemala, Buenos Aires, Chile, and toured around in South America.

She finally arrived in Houston, where, true to their promise, the di Portanovas received her in style and treated her like royalty. The generous-hearted Texans took to her at once and arranged for her to visit the top of the secret Gemini spaceship control centre at nearby Clear Lake City, where she met leading American astronauts. She was also given the freedom of the city of Houston. The mayor presented her with a golden key and parchment scroll, saying, 'The freedom of our city is given only to rather special people. The Duchess's arrival created a fantastic stir here. In terms of the number of parties held, her impact was bigger than the Beatles. We feel that to give her the freedom of our city was the least we could do to show our admiration.'

The following year she was on the move again when she accepted an invitation to stay in Colombo, Ceylon, now Sri Lanka. She travelled on to Nepal and, after flying to Cambodia via Bangkok, realized that she very much missed Bill, who had made her travel arrangements so easy in the past.

On her return to London, though, she found that he didn't miss her half as much as she had missed him. He had decided to end the relationship and to return to his wife. He didn't have the heart to tell her so, but instead sent her a letter explaining that although he found her one of the most beautiful and exciting women he had ever met, it really was goodbye. He thanked her for the six-year relationship and she never heard from him again. Margaret, a born survivor, had no alternative but to pick herself up and start again.

She managed to break several of her father's trusts in order to maintain her lifestyle, but she still had her stepmother's claim on the property in Nassau to contend with. 'I'm going to have to pay her,' Margaret finally admitted when she discovered that Jane Whigham had succeeded in her claim to the property in the Bahamas under its dower law. And then switching away from all things legal, she went on, 'I don't want people to think that even after the divorce I spent all my time in the law courts. That was bad enough. I want them to think, "Here comes a brand-new woman." After the divorce was over, I want them to know that I never changed my life. I went on living. I travelled enormously.' At that point of the conversation, she looked towards the door. One of her poodles had entered with a woman's hat in its mouth. 'Oh, there's Baby with Mrs Duckworth's hat.' She laughed tenderly. The dog rushed towards her. She leant down from her comfortable arm-chair, scooped it up and caressed it lovingly. This gesture illustrated an element of tenderness and caring, hitherto alien to her nature.

Then she began to talk about the major charitable involvements that had occupied the next few years of her life. First, in July 1968, she joined a campaign to save the Argyll and Sutherland Highlanders. She had read news of the proposal to disband the Argylls' battalion, headed by Colonel Colin Mitchell. 'I was on a trip to Norway, a sort of cruise trip in July sixty-eight,' Margaret began, 'and when I came back I read that the Argyll and Sutherland Highlanders were going to be axed. I was very upset because I'd got a cousin in the Argylls. They were going to be axed for economy reasons. I thought my ex-husband, Ian Argyll, would be in there pitching for them because he was a captain in the Argylls during the war, and he was also a prisoner-of-war as an Argyll. And then I called up the press who I knew had been talking to him about it, and they replied, "Yes, we have talked to the Duke about this, and he just answered, 'Look, please don't bother me about this any more. Don't call me any more. I'm not interested.'" And this gave me the go-ahead. I mean, if he was doing it, I would have pretty well bowed out. So I then called up General Sir Gordon Macmillan who was leading the thing, and I said, "Could I help from

London?" I knew they were all signing the petition like mad five times each up in Scotland, and he said, "Yes. We would be very grateful." In the meantime, I got hold of Colin Mitchell who was the one getting all the press. He was called "Mad Mitch" because he did mad things. He was a compulsive rebel who did mad things, and was a leader who got people to follow him. The stories about him in Aden are simply hilarious. But he was the one who I knew would get the attention of the public, and he did. I said I would do whatever they wanted me to do. They wanted names for the petition, not money. They wanted a million signatures. Which is a lot of signatures. Against this axing. The Argylls wouldn't amalgamate with any other regiment. They said, "We stand, or fall alone." And they were very tough about it and everybody in Scotland was signing it without any trouble, but Scotland isn't a very big country. So I put a notice in *The Times* to say that if anybody would like to sign the petition here in London, would they contact me at Scotch House, which is in the Brompton Road, opposite Harrods. I'd be there on a certain day, from eleven to five, and I'd take signatures and start the ball rolling. And then they all came. Young Iona, Ian's young daughter-in-law, was one of the first to arrive, which was very nice of her.' (Here Margaret switched from the regiment to her dogs, who had become troublesome. 'All right, Alphonse,' she said to the poodle, 'if you want to get down [from the sofa], get down. I'm sorry. I'm sorry, Baby.' The dog growled. 'A little—' she stammered. 'A tiny protest. He's trodden on by the others because they don't see him. They're blind. This tape is going to sound very queer,' she added, referring to our recorded conversation.

'So,' she returned to the Argyll campaign, 'the people came in droves to sign the petition in London. We got a lot of press and television and a lot of notice was taken, which is what we wanted. It was a tremendous campaign, and, of course, a lot of people were anti it, because they had their own regiments, and they were saying, "Why the Argylls? Why not the Norfolk Yeomanry, or something? What about us?" All this happened in July, August and September. Then I gave a luncheon for Colin Mitchell in October. He had a terribly tough time with the army. He ought to be a brigadier by now. But he was a rebel and would not be told, so they didn't make him a brigadier. And then he resigned in a huff. They were terrified of him. They were terrified of *me*. They were terrified of us both, up in Scotland at Headquarters. They didn't know what was going to hit them next. But we had to get the publicity, to get the people. You can't get a campaign without publicity. And he was an absolute star figure. If he went anywhere in ordinary clothes he was recognized. He was loved. And he was a very good speaker. Every time he spoke on television, up went the signatures. He was a sort of star.

'But I thought he was a sort of wounded figure. And so I had the luncheon here. I had about fifty-four people in that dining room, which is a lot of people. I had people from all walks of life. I had a lot of the Cabinet, a lot of politicians, a lot of press. I had Max Aitken, Vere Harmsworth and I had Charles Winter. I also had Peter Bull. I forget who Peter Bull was, but I had him here. [He was a well-known actor.] There was also Jocelyn Stevens who became managing director of Beaverbrook Newspapers, also Lord Thomson of Fleet. But they all came as private individuals. It was a very impressive list and it was in *The Times* and the *Daily Telegraph* officially, in the Court Circulars.

'But by then we'd only had 500,000 signatures, and we needed a million. So then I called up Sir Gordon and said, "Please, have you asked the Commonwealth for signatures?" He was the one who started the campaign. There was also a man called George Younger. He was the other one who started it. Also Gordon Campbell, and Hugh Fraser, Lord Lovat's brother. He was an MP. All Scots.

'So I found out how to do it. I called up Associated Press and said to them, "Could you get a message through to the press of all the Commonwealth countries?" And they said, "We can do it within an hour. Tell us what you want to say."'

Entering into the spirit of the campaign, and showing the enterprising skill for organizing and management which she had applied to both herself and her personal pursuits all her life, she led them valiantly. They managed to get the support of the Commonwealth countries, and burnt the midnight oil sending out the petition forms. Each form had room for twenty-five signatures, and they were dutifully returned, with signatures. But there were still not enough, so Margaret turned to the Scots in America. 'I could have got a million signatures from America alone. Easily. Odd pockets. Not New York. Not Washington. But California and Cincinnati signed to a man. Detroit and Burbank, California, signed to a man. Strange pockets. San Diego. A great many St Andrew's Clubs. Thistle Clubs. Scots names. But then we had to stop. Like the theatre, you must draw the curtain down. And they closed it at about Christmastime. And then we had a hilarious time. Twenty-two whisky cartons arrived from Scotland, put on a train, labelled SAVE THE ARGYLLS. There were four generals on the train to escort them down. We were all on the platform at Euston, to meet this train. I can't tell you what it was like. It was like a Keystone comedy. The train broke down, and it was about an hour late. And in that time, the generals had got sloshed. A lot of our people were sloshed and off they unloaded two Securicor cars full with a piper playing, and he, too, was absolutely sloshed to the gills. The cartons were taken to the vaults of the Houses of Parliament where they were kept until the petition was actually made. You have to make a petition to the Houses of Parliament.

It isn't any good just signing. So then Colin Mitchell and I went to watch this performance. In came two men, side by side, with a box each, and they put them in front of the Speaker, and went back for two more. They made eleven trips! There were cheers from the Right. And boos from the Left. Harold Wilson didn't want it to go through. In the end the whole thing was resolved, but the company only had one hundred and twenty, so they were allowed to stay on. But they were told that they had to get a battalion force again. So then they had to recruit. I'm told that they literally had to knock people on the head and say, "You're now an *Argyll*." Within a month or two they got it up from a hundred and twenty men to over nine hundred. And so they became a full battalion. And nobody will ever, ever try and axe them again. And they deserved it because they were stars. The Argylls were the stars of all the regiments who were included on the petition forms. They had a fantastic record all over the world. And they had just been in Aden and done a terrific job there.'

But even though Margaret had achieved her aim in helping to save the Argylls she still had an axe to grind regarding her ex-husband: 'Ian should have done something for the regiment, for God's sake. He should have done what I did. He never raised a finger. Never moved a muscle. And I think it was because of lethargy. I think it's the egg and the chicken syndrome. Drink makes lethargy, and lethargy makes drink. You don't know which comes first. It was hard to get him to put his signature to paper. And it was a short signature. During our marriage I would be saying, when it came to signing something for charity, "Listen, I'll sign them *for* you, but for God's sake, sign them *yourself.*" And I was up against this inertia all our married life. I mean, I used to find him asleep on the sofa at three in the afternoon. Drove me out of my mind. Anyway, he should have done this, and he didn't. So I did. I didn't do it all. I only did the part that wasn't Scotland.'

Taking up good causes was seen by her as a way of making amends for a scandalous divorce. However, old habits die hard and even in her later years Margaret did not allow conventional morality to stand in her way. But she had learnt a lesson: never be found out.

She was excluded from any gathering, whether formal or not, at which British royalty would be present, and this, too, narrowed her field.

Having been abandoned by her husband, her former lovers, the man with whom she was in love for the six years after her divorce, as well as her daughter and her grandchildren, it would appear that there was little of substance left in life for her. But aside from her strong feelings for animals, children and, inevitably, the Argyll regiment for which she fought so strongly, what incensed her most? 'Cruelty to anything,' she said without hesitation or stammer. 'Children and animals. Cruelty to anybody helpless. Anything that can't fight back.'

And what gave her the greatest happiness? 'That's a very big question,' she replied. And then after a long pause while she thought on it, she said, 'Well, a tremendous pleasure of mine is travelling. I don't say I want to travel all the year round. But when I go off on a long trip, I'm very happy. And I'm very happy to come home. But travel is a tremendously important thing in my life.'

She had, of course, mistaken 'travel' for 'escape'. When the pressures and the burdens of her life and the dishar-mony and discord she created around her became too overwhelming, she realized that she had to remove herself. She needed cooling-off periods. Time away from home was essential. She had to find new friends and new places. She wanted to enjoy the warmth and friendship of new acquaintances and forget about her unhappiness. She had always had a charismatic personality and she knew that she would be welcome wherever she went. She was the object of many people's desire and admiration, and she, more than anyone, knew how to use it to the full. She was also conscious of her curiosity value. Heads would turn when she entered a room. In that same vein of self-deceit and fantasy, as if grasping for the last vestiges of human kindness, she revealed a part of the heart that beat beneath the cool façade.

'All my life I had a dream, even as a child. A dream of having a home for old horses and dogs that are lost or distressed or who are hurt. In this dream I had kennel-maids dressed in white, and I was in a big house surrounded by lots of parks and fields. All the kennels and stables I needed for the animals were there. I had this absolute dream. This mirage, as a child. I had this great dream of always looking after animals but that was as far as it got. And all of a sudden, before it hit the press in 1968, that dream was fulfilled. It was the strangest thing. You talk about fate…'

And then she explained how that dream came true.

CHAPTER ELEVEN

Good Causes

T HE end of the sixties showed Margaret in a completely new light. Her character was transformed and she began to show the caring side of her nature. She started giving instead of taking. But for all that, she still had one eye on self-glorification. Her desire for public recognition and adoration took a different form. Early in January 1968 she received one of many appeals in the post. She had, until now, thrown begging letters in the waste-paper basket, but something about this one from Lancashire, which was headed SAVE THESE ANIMALS, made her read on.

'The pamphlet that arrived in the post had pictures all round the page of all these animals. Horses, dogs, donkeys,' she related, her stammer holding her back from proceeding too quickly in her enthusiasm to recall the appeal. 'Just animals. It said, "Please save these animals, and if you don't, they're just going to die." I read the thing, and cried for one hour. And I was about to write a cheque for everything I own. And then I thought, "Now pull yourself together, Margaret, and be sensible. You must call the RSPCA," I told myself. And I called them up and said, "Do you know about an animal sanctuary which is called Bleakholt, which is up in Lancashire?" "Oh, we know about it." They said that they were in very bad trouble. It is tremendously overcrowded, and they were very worried about it. "The woman over there is quite extraordinary. She's a very dedicated woman. A Mrs Lomas. She's got the heart, but she hasn't got the managerial experience to run this place. But the animals are always well fed, and they're under a roof. However, it's chaos." So I got this idea in my head, and said, "Listen, could you have your regional officer meet me up there to come with me to see this place, because I've got to have somebody to hang on to my coat-tails to stop me from handing over to them everything I have. And crying. Somebody's got to come over with me. To control me. So could you have your" – his name was Mr Goodenough, as it happens – "could he please meet me and take me over there and could you please tell me what I could do that is constructive. Except me crying. That isn't going to do anybody any good."

'So I went up to a friend of mine who has got a house up in Yorkshire, and he was very anti this place. And I began to get my hackles up on the drive over, because as soon as somebody's anti something, I'm apt to, being a Scot, go the other way.

'"Of course this place should be shut down," he said. "They're keeping a circus pony there who's a freak. It should be shot. The place is a disgrace."

'So I said, "Well, let's go and see it. I'm only going because it's in trouble. If it was absolutely fine and dandy I wouldn't *be* here. I want you to tell me what can be done constructively, not just keep saying, 'It's awful.'"

'We got there, and I must say, Mrs Lomas was – actually, it was a farmhouse, in a very bleak, open moor. It's the bleakest, ugliest place I've ever seen, and I loved it. It's quite a big farm. It's got about thirty acres. And it was packed with animals. You heard them. You saw them. They were in every corner. In every shed. Every nook or cranny had a dog or cat in it. In mud, in confusion. And I must say, Mrs Lomas endeared herself to me. She was quite a young woman, with a very nice face. She said, "I'm not going to apologize for anything, because I just can't begin to apologize. I'm just going to show you." She was a very outgoing, outspoken woman. Tremendously warmhearted, and she obviously adored animals. And I said, "Look, I don't want apologies. I've come to help because I got your appeal."

And she said, "Well, how you got it I don't know, because we never send the appeals to London." This was an act of God. Nobody ever knew who sent this appeal to me. They had about three thousand people all over the area who supported them, but no one in London, and, by some strange quirk of fate, I got this.

'And we went all over it, and I said, "Now, Mr Good-enough mentioned a circus pony." And she said, "Oh, Jackie. I'll show you Jackie." So then we saw dear Jackie, who was a circus pony, and who *was* a freak. But was only a freak in that he had tiny legs. He had a perfectly full-grown body, but with these tiny legs. Like a Shetland pony. But the legs weren't bent or buckled. He could support himself perfectly well, and he was a darling.

'So I said to Mr Goodenough, "You want to have *that* shot? I'll shoot *you*." And he said, "Well, he looks much better than he did." So I said, "Well, he stays alive for one." And then I said, "Tell me about this and this and this." Well, of course, everything was obviously wrong. Everything. Including no money. So I said, "Look, I'm going to take this under my wing and try to put it right." And Mrs Lomas replied, "Well, this is like manna from heaven for us. We were at the end of our tether." When I came into it, they were about to put down five hundred animals. I kept on sending money. I would want it to build thirty kennels, for instance, but the kennels were never built because she was using the money to pay the butcher and all the other suppliers instead. No accounts were kept and she began to get a terribly bad reputation for not paying the bills. She was an extraordinary money-raiser. I've never known anybody get money out of a stone the way she did. She raised something like twenty-five thousand pounds a year, but they were spending thirty thousand. It was the old Mr Micawber all over again. And then I discovered that nobody was being paid. She owed money to the vet, the lawyer and to everybody else. They were all working for nothing to keep this place going. Everybody. And at least the animals were not on an open road, ready to be killed.

'There was a tremendous amount of mange and enteritis. I kept sending this money, and getting nowhere. So I got the Charity Commissioners here in London in my drawing room, as well as the Bleakholt lawyer, and said, "Look, I beg you to register this place as an official charity. I'll guarantee it. I know there's every single thing wrong you can think of but they're in debt. We haven't any accounts to show you, and we won't have for two years. It's chaotic, but please, please, please, make it a registered charity, because until you do I can't get money, and I can't support it unless it's a registered charity. It's the only thing that gives it the stamp of approval."

'The man was sweet. He said, "That's what we're here for. To help. We've got a big map here of charities all over the country, and we'll put you on the map." And I said, "Yes, but when do we move up an inch or two?" He said, "As a rule, it takes a year." I said, "It's not going to take a year. It will take a month. Come on." And he said to the lawyer, "You'll have to draft out something. I'll read it." I said, "Look. What are we here for? You're going to draft this thing together *now*. And I'm going to read this *Daily Express* in this room while you're doing it." I told him that this lawyer hadn't come all this way from Lancashire for nothing. So they drafted this thing together, which pleased them both, and the thing was done. And, to cut a long story short, it was an official registered charity within six weeks. We formulated a very good committee and got an excellent chairman. And then I began to appeal in the *Daily Telegraph*, and we began to get a lot of money in. We also got legacies, because, funnily enough, we advertised in the *New Law Journal*, and that did it. It's the best thing to appeal in because you get legacies. People scratching out their children from their wills!

'Every single penny that comes in now is accounted for, but it took a long time to do. We began to get a very good press, because we were taking in pit ponies, and the Blackpool ponies which were tired out. And old horses come to stay to the end of their lives. We let animals out to homes, but we keep a very firm eye on the homes. We don't let dogs or cats go into a flat, for instance. In our charter it says that no animal would ever be turned away, but we've had to cool that down a bit, because people would come and say, "Look, take this puppy, we're bored with it." And we say, "Come back in ten days' time and in the meantime see if you can find a home for it yourself."

'Now everybody's very proud of Bleakholt, including me. Before, they were ashamed of it. It's a great success, thank God.'

But although she had won the admiration of animal lovers, and the mute gratitude of the animals themselves, no doubt, for her strenuous efforts to save the sanctuary, she came under fire when she stuck her neck out next time in her role as saviour.

Saving the animals could not, and did not, fill the void left when she realized that she would never again see her grandchildren. Whether it was a deep need to show her latent love to some other deserving children or to punish her daughter for discarding her so finally, she decided to adopt a child, a boy. And all hell was let loose.

She put this extraordinary decision down to another dream. It is unlikely that dreams had any place in her night-time activities, but the whole thing turned into a nightmare when the press got hold of her plan. And half the nation rebelled.

'The other dream I had as a child was to adopt six orphans. From, probably, India or somewhere. I wasn't very practical in my dreams,' she said. 'I wanted to look after six very hungry, starving orphans from under-privileged countries. Of course nothing happened about that. It remained in my dreams. But I honestly thought at the time of Biafra of having a child sent over from there. I thought about it quite often, and then I felt it wasn't really fair to bring a child over and give it such a change, and also I wasn't prepared to have the whole nursery business again, you know, at my age. I'd done it all. I wanted to do something about children and I didn't quite know how to go about it. I've got a friend who is a priest. Actually, he's a very well-known priest now. He's called Father Andrew. He was chaplain to the Archbishop of Canterbury for nine years. Then he became Vicar of Preston. And now he's Rector of St Thomas's Church in New York, which is the second-richest church in America. He is very young, only forty-two, and he's very bright. So I talked about this to him, and I talked about it to a headmaster I knew at a school in Warwickshire. He had asked me to be their governor, which I am. The school is called Kinwarton-in-Warwick, and a dear little school, which is unsubsidized and unhelped. It's for children up to eleven. I helped them because they were getting no help from the Government at all. I said to Mr Rutter, who was the headmaster, he was a darling: "Look out for a boy who is poor, and intelligent." I mean, I didn't want an idiot. "Find a boy who hasn't got the chance to have the education that he should have. And if he gets it, he will make the most of it. And I will try and help him." And I then said the same thing to Father Andrew because they both work with children. I said, "I want to take him under my wing. I want to help, but I don't know how. Because my grandchildren have got everything on earth. If one wants to give them a tape recorder, or a camera, they've got eight of them already. You can't help them, they've got so much. They've got so many aunts and uncles, and they've got adoring parents – you can't give them anything."

'So everybody kept an eye open, and I didn't do much about it, and then Mr Rutter said, "I think I've got a boy. But he's got a brother." So I said, "Then we'll have to take the two of them. We can't take one."

'Their father had been a sort of dropout. He had been at Oxford, and he was a dropout. The mother was the second wife who had these two little boys. She had the most terrible struggle. She was a teacher, and they just hadn't any money. They hadn't any money at all. They were living on his pension. These two boys were going to grammar school, and learning nothing. They were very bright boys, and getting nowhere. And this is what I wanted, you see. So I met them. They were terribly sweet, and well mannered. Dear little boys. Very nicely dressed. Very polite. Dear little boys. At that point they were about seven and nine. God knows, it's all in the newspaper cuttings. And so I said I would adopt them. And everybody said, "Why use the word adopt?" But it's the only word in the English language to cover it. Sponsor is an American word. You have to take out adoption papers, and this is what the fuss was about. And I said, "I will guarantee to look after their education, their health, and in every way I can, except have them live with me, until they are twenty-one." I would love to take them away on trips with me when they are older, you know?

'So generally, in a way, and in actual fact, I adopted them, but they would continue to live with their mother. It's an odd word, but it's the only word. There are adoption papers in existence, even now, over these two children. And, of course, the press got hold of this. I thought, I should take them to Kinwarton (a private prep school) because otherwise people would think what the hell am I doing with two little boys at my age? Who are they? Are they two illegitimate grandchildren? So I took them officially to Kinwarton, to introduce them to the headmaster, who of course knew about them. And the press got hold of this and did a sort of blitz on us. The boys began their schooling at Kinwarton and then all hell broke loose.

'They must have thought I was an axe-murderess. Questions were asked in Parliament as to how she can adopt children at her age without a husband. Mr Leo Abse got up and said, "This is a disgrace." And the press were swarming around their house. Their school. Like ants. For four days. And *this* house. And they got the father into a pub, and they got him tight. And he gave them the most hair-raising interview, saying, "This is wonderful news for my children. Now I can drink Scotch instead of beer," and "oh!" and "I am glad." And this upped it. And I had to put in the papers that we all signed, that they would never, never speak to the press again. Because I knew they were being offered a hundred, two hundred, three hundred pounds by *Paris Match*. By *Life* magazine. By all of them, for the story. I had put in the documents that if they did speak to the press again the deal was off. I mean, it was torture. But *now*, it has turned out just as I meant it to. One boy has moved on to a school, Bedstone, which is a charming school, on the very borders of Wales, Shropshire. They come up during their holidays for two or three days at a time to see me. They're eleven and thirteen now. Funnily enough, I got two letters from them today, which I kept.'

She left the room to find the letters, and returned presently to read them out. She explained that they had visited her the week before. "'Thank you for the day out, and for taking us to see *The Mousetrap*,'" Margaret read from young Richard's letter. "'It was the best show I've ever seen in my life. I thought it was wonderful. Now I know why it has been running for twenty-two years. Very excited about the Canadian holiday. Thank you for letting me go." He's going on a Canadian holiday, because the school arranges these holidays, which is marvellous. Austria, then Switzerland and to Canada with the master, which is heaven for them.' And then reading from the other letter: 'That's the letter from the little one, Jamie. I gave him a bicycle. "Thank you for the lovely time we had on Wednesday. I enjoyed it all very much, and especially going to Harrods and choosing my bicycle. I can't wait for it to come."

'Rather sweet,' Margaret commented on the letter. 'Well, Jamie's rather out of it because he's not getting the trip, so I thought we must make it up to him with the bike. It will be, in a way, rather exciting, if one or the other became a great doctor, or a great scientist or something, wouldn't it? I mean, I don't think they'll be dropouts. They've got a very nice mother. A terribly sweet mother. Who has had a very tough time. So it would be very rewarding if one of them at least turned out to be something really rather special, wouldn't it? Perhaps either an artist, or a singer. I think they'll get scholarships to Oxford. But after they reach the age of twenty-one, I end.'

Leo Abse, however, felt that Margaret wasn't morally fit to be responsible for two young needy children. In 1970 he represented Labour, in Pontypool, and put forward a motion to ask Mrs Thatcher, the then Minister of Education, if she was aware that a headmaster was acting as an intermediary in a form of the adoption in respect of the Gardner boys, Richard and Jamie. Mr Abse, a solicitor, said, 'It seems in this case that no adjudicating body has inquired into the suitability of the Duchess with regard to the adoption of the two boys.'

In the meantime, Margaret told the boys' father that if he had anything more to say to the press about her plans, she would withdraw her support. She had already set up the trust fund for the boys, and when taxed by the press for more information the boys' father, Howard Gardner, said guardedly, 'I am not prepared to clear up any mystery about who the adoptive parent is. If I step out of line the Duchess will cancel the agreement. That has been made perfectly clear to me.'

She was determined to keep her name on the marquee, in bright, shiny lights, no matter what device she might employ. She knew that she had to sustain the public's interest. She fed on it. 'I am born under the sign of Sagittarius,' Margaret said. 'I'm Sagittarian. I love people. I love travel.'

In 1971 she pursued her love of travel by taking another trip to America. This time, she visited Washington, where she spent ten days with Perle Mesta who took her along to the Senate to hear President Nixon deliver his State of the Union Message at the opening of Congress. She also met White House dignitaries, senators, congressmen and their wives, and returned to London where she learnt that, at long last, she had emerged with £58,000 from the legal battle over her father's estate in the Bahamas. Under her 'dower right', however, Jane was still entitled to a third share of the Caribbean estate.

Margaret also discovered that moves were being made by the Duke's old friend Lord Cecil Douglas to have him brought back to the bosom of White's, London's oldest and most exclusive club. By now, he and Mathilda, the fourth Duchess, were living in their apartment in Paris for tax reasons, and the Duke had put word abroad that he would like to return to his old club. Margaret promptly telephoned her friends and ensured that his social exile continued.

Shortly after hearing this news, Margaret visited Paris where she stayed at the Ritz. She dined with her old friend J. Paul Getty, and then, seated at a table on his own, she noticed the Duke. They looked at one another across the room, and after a flicker of recognition, they avoided any further exchange. It was the last time she ever saw him.

The Duke suffered a stroke early in 1973 in France. He was flown to the Western General Hospital in Edinburgh and put into a public ward, but he died shortly afterwards at the age of sixty-nine. Only hours before the Duke's death, Scottish Labour MP Willie Hamilton protested in the House of Commons at the Duke's being admitted to hospital as a National Health patient after leaving the country to avoid tax. The Marquess of Lorne, now Duke of Argyll, pointed out, however, that the family had paid substantial taxes over many years, and death duties of about £750,000.

When Margaret heard of her ex-husband's death it was as though a heavy mantle had been lifted from her shoulders. She felt strangely free. The sensation led her to invite me to write her memoirs shortly after the Duke's death. She felt free to disclose the intimate secrets of their marriage without fear of redress. She knew that the dead can't sue. Margaret and I organized a party at her Mayfair house to celebrate the launch of the book, *Famous Faces*, published by Arnold Weissberger, the American theatrical lawyer who had first introduced me to Margaret in his New York apartment the year before. The guest list of around fifty people included Lady Diana Cooper, one of the women Margaret had looked up to. Margaret had become known among her stepchildren as Snow White's vain, wicked stepmother, who, upon gazing at herself in the glass, asks, 'Mirror, mirror on the wall, who is the fairest of them all?' When Lady Diana was told one day that I had seen Margaret recently, quick as a flash, she asked: 'And how is "Mirror, Mirror"?' The other guests included Dame Alicia Markova, Sir Cecil Beaton, film director John Schlesinger, playwright Tom Stoppard, Lauren Bacall, Ann Todd, Dinah Sheridan, Mrs Boris Karloff, Mrs Jack Hawkins and Brian Sweeny, her son.

After most people had left, a young woman picked up an elegant satin cushion from the sofa and plonked it on the floor. She settled into it, threw back her head and said, 'What a fun party, Margaret. Let's swap gossip.'

Margaret looked down at her coldly and replied, 'It's not that sort of party. And it's not that sort of cushion.'

The woman replaced it and apologized. She left soon after.

Moira Lister saw the funny side at a different party Margaret had given at Upper Grosvenor Street: 'She invited us all to dinner, and there was no butler. The cook or the maid brought in the food. One or two of the guests had to get up and help with the serving and when we left the dinner table and went into the drawing room, Margaret said: "I'm frightfully sorry. But the butler passed out just five minutes before dinner. I'm afraid that I had nowhere else to put him but he has actually been under the dinner table all this time." None of us knew, but we had this lovely dinner with him flat out under the table!' By the time he sobered up in the morning he didn't remember a thing.

Shortly after the publication party, Margaret and I came to blows. I had prepared a synopsis of over 20,000 words, a considerable length for any synopsis, and had offered it to my publishers, then W. H. Allen who were noted for publishing books with media interest. They had published my two previous biographies entitled *This Was Richard Tauber* and *Noël*, a biography about Sir Noël Coward, and had invited me to write and produce a television documentary film about the Duchess of Bedford to coincide with the publication of her memoirs, *Nicole Nobody*. The publishers had an option on my next book and I was therefore obliged to offer them the Margaret Argyll book. When they had read the synopsis, an advance payment of £25,000 was discussed. It had been suggested in the early stages that Margaret and I were to share all proceeds from the project on a straight fifty/fifty basis. The publisher, Jeffrey Simmons, dined with Margaret and me, examined the recorded tapes I had made and saw the bound books of press cuttings Margaret had collected through the years. He told us that he would be prepared to go ahead with the book and would draft an agreement.

However, before an agreement could be formalized, Margaret, herself not willing to give away half the royalties, and the publishers, now directly in communication with the Duchess, decided to proceed with the book under another writer. All my hard work to initiate the project was bypassed and, reluctantly, I saw my planned book proceed under someone else's name and with no share of its success or proceeds. I felt I had been the victim of an underhand plot hatched by the publishers and Margaret, a view I expressed to Margaret in a letter having failed to get through to her by phone.

I explained to you that as I had an agreement with my own publishers I would have to offer my next work to them, and you agreed that we should send them the synopsis when it was completed. This I did, they accepted it, and I brought my publisher, Jeffrey Simmons, along to meet you and we dined together. The three of us discussed the project, Jeffrey intimated that he would like to proceed with the book, and nothing could have surprised me more than to find that shortly after you met him privately behind my back to discuss terms.

However, my protests were to no avail and they proceeded without me.

They were, sadly, the last of the parties she was to give at home. The money her father had left was drying up, and the income of £18,000 a year from a UK trust fund was not enough to cover her extravagant lifestyle. A butler, a cook, a housekeeper, a chauffeur, two maids and a couture wardrobe were essentials she could not sacrifice.

Then Margaret had the bright idea of opening her home to the public, at £7.50 a head. For this, visitors, mostly American, would be shown the sights, given a glass of champagne and have the pleasure of meeting her. She had planned to greet the tourists three evenings a week, thirty at a time. 'We all have to change our way of life these days,' she explained. 'Even duchesses feel the draught.' But she was apprehensive about her landlord, the Duke of Westminster. It was, after all, a leased house. Her father had made it over to her, together with two mews houses at the back, in 1946 with thirty-one years left to go, but time was running out fast. She knew that to renew the lease would be cripplingly expensive, with inflation and rising rates, and this new venture she hoped would be a chance of survival.

She planned to receive her guests descending the cantilevered stairs in clouds of diaphanous pale peach chiffon, a white fox-fur collar and the three strands of pearls which she never took off. Equipped with all the grace and serenity of the worldly duchess persona that she had cultivated throughout the years, and with the aura of the cinema star she had always dreamed of being, she was ready for the curtain to rise.

Several ambassadors were invited to the private launch in April 1975, but only those from France, Switzerland, Sweden, Turkey and Norway arrived. No one was present from either the USA or Japan, with whose countrymen she had hoped to fill the house. One of her ex-lovers, Lord Duncan Sandys, made an early exit. He had seen it all many times before – but in more intimate circumstances.

Vincent Shaw, her business manager, who had also arranged Sooty exhibitions, spoke kind words and courtesies to members of the press and photographers.

As the press and the posh departed, Margaret stood at the hall door with her two black poodles nestling at her size-three feet. Sammy the budgerigar chirped away gaily upstairs in her little library, impervious to his mistress's *folies de grandeur*. She thanked them for attending and hoped they would bang the drum. But few paying visitors attended after the official bash. The writing was on the wall.

The curtain had come down.

Margaret had had a long run, but it was time to move on. Where to go?

Money was no longer in abundance. She had been ostracized by her family. The players and orchestra had left. The audience had cleared the house before the set was struck, and she was growing old. Would she, like one of her idols of the silent screen, Gloria Swanson, return in a remake of *Sunset Boulevard*? Before vacating the house she tried one last time to relive the old glamorous days with an extravagant party given at the Dorchester for John Paul Getty's eightieth birthday. King Umberto of Italy travelled from his villa in Portugal as did the Spanish royal family. Patricia Nixon, daughter of the US President in those glorious pre-Watergate days, arrived from Washington with the US Ambassador. The Duke of Bedford came from Paris and countless members of the jet set from all over the world enjoyed the extravagant flower arrangements flown in from Madrid by an admirer, the orchestra, and exquisite food and champagne.

For a woman having for the first time in her life to make economies, this elaborate display of opulence was a sad charade.

CHAPTER TWELVE

The Beginning of the End

T HE Grosvenor House in Park Lane is one of the most prestigious hotels in London. The magnificent site has been famous for hospitality on a grand scale for three centuries. Richard, the first Earl Grosvenor, made the old Grosvenor House his London residence in 1732 and set about creating a grand household. He built the first Grosvenor Gallery for his magnificent collection of paintings, to house masterpieces including Gainsborough's *Blue Boy.*

In 1927 the new Grosvenor House was built on the site of the old one. Sir Edwin Lutyens, the architect, provided the design, and work began on two large blocks. One contained luxury service flats, and the other became the first hotel in Park Lane. It was here, in the style to which she had been born and been accustomed, that Margaret spent the next twelve years of her life when she left her house round the corner.

The publication of her autobiography, entitled *Forget Not*, in which she told about half the story of her life, was not the success she had hoped for. Although she was paid £22,000 in advance of royalties, it was ghosted by at least three writers who saw little of the money. It was clear that she had become increasingly hard up and needed every penny she could find.

When Margaret realized that she could not afford to renew the lease on her house, she turned to Lord Forte, chairman of the massive Trust House Forte empire. He reigned over a domain of over six hundred hotels, and catering outlets on motorways and airports. Although other top London hotels owned by the group included Brown's, the Hyde Park Hotel and the Westbury, since the fashionable Grosvenor House was situated just round the corner from her house in Upper Grosvenor Street, it seemed the most likely choice. Margaret wanted to stay in the neighbourhood that was familiar to her. She chose a penthouse apartment on the eighth floor, number 148. (Her own address, by coincidence, had been 48.) It consisted of a large, elegant drawing room, two bedrooms with bathrooms, a kitchen, and an additional bedroom and bathroom used by her live-in maid.

It overlooks Hyde Park, and Margaret was seen daily, taking her poodles for walks. This duty fell to her maid when the animals wanted to be taken out at least three times a day.

The rent for the apartment was £30,000 a year, but Lord Forte allowed Margaret to have it at £20,000 a year because he considered she would lend glamour to the hotel. At £400 a week, or less than £60 a day, she could not have done better.

Some of her furniture was moved into the apartment, and she turned the second bedroom into a dressing room. It was big enough to accommodate her exquisite couture dresses made by Worth, Balenciaga, Hartnell and Dior, each in their individual plastic zip covers all of which she had kept throughout the years. An entire wall was needed for her shoes alone, each with its neat shoe tree and flannel covers for travel. Her underwear was kept in satin envelopes monogrammed with her initials and coronet. There were also forty handmade hairpieces in subtly differing tones, all kept on their own wooden stands. There were index cards to help her dresser which were kept inside each dress cover and referred to the matching handbag, gloves, shoes, wrap or coat as well as to the number of the hairpiece that best matched the colour. Even during periods of her most stringent economy, Mancini shoes from Paris costing 'only' £350 per pair under a special arrangement were still being made to match a particular dress.

When she first moved into the apartment in 1978, she continued with the idea she had at Upper Grosvenor Street and opened it to the public, charging the odd amount of £15.95 for the privilege of looking round. This included the pleasure of meeting Margaret, but tourists paid extra for her book which she signed 'Love Margaret'.

The management were aware of this ruse, and played along with it. Included in the price was a glass of Buck's Fizz but she always used sparkling wine instead of champagne, with plenty of orange juice. If anyone asked for anything different they were told it was not included in the tour. On one occasion, standing among the visitors who were watching fireworks in Hyde Park from her window, Margaret's hairpiece was noticeably dislodging itself. While the head waiter discreetly tried to attract her attention, a less discreet Italian waiter on duty shouted rather loudly, 'Your Grace! Your wig is walking!' Margaret calmly left the room to adjust it and re-entered without batting an eyelid.

Margaret's tenure at Grosvenor House lasted until 1990. During that time, the general manager, Tony Murkett, saw her frequently. A dark-haired, charming man with an engaging smile and exquisite manners, it was not surprising that Margaret took to him immediately. Having worked in several of the group's other hotels for many years, he arrived at the Grosvenor House as deputy general manager. Then the general manager was Pierre Vacher, but it was part of Tony's job to act as troubleshooter. 'At her early evening cocktail parties we were only required to supply celery with cottage cheese,' Tony said. He naturally respected the confidences of the guests who stayed at the hotel, but he was a close observer of the activities of all who entered its portals. 'It was rather frugal.' He laughed. She always drank white wine, maintaining that champagne disagreed with her digestion and although the white wine chosen was usually good the champagne, which she was unlikely to touch, was invariably the cheapest available and bought directly from the wine merchants which worked out far cheaper than the hotel's. Her parties still attracted everybody who was asked and she always prided herself that people came for the company rather than for the food.

Even though there was a kitchen in the apartment and she had her own maid, Margaret hardly ever utilized them for dinner parties, preferring the more costly alternative of eating in one of the three restaurants in the hotel.

'She had lots of visitors. Young chaps. Young men.' Tony Murkett was too discreet to comment, but, by and large, they were gay. They would feed her ego, saying to her, 'Darling, you're divine. You're a star.' The more manly ones would be out chasing younger damsels.

Moira Lister recalls, 'She did not entertain there a lot, but went out a great deal.'

Moira Lister was not convinced that she was as promiscuous as others might have believed. 'All that business with the lovers.' She sighed. 'Of course, I'm not a man so I couldn't say. But she always seemed so austere and cold. She always had this "Don't touch me. Don't disarrange me" aura about her. So how did she manage all these lovers? How did they get through that icy façade? I've known her all these years and seen her so many times. But she didn't seem particularly flirtatious with men. She didn't seem to be sensuous. She wasn't sensual in an apparent way. I used to watch her very closely, very often, and I used to think, If I were a man I'd be rather frightened to approach you. She always kept her dignity. She was an enormously dignified lady. She really was a special person. Admittedly, she had her eccentricities. But she loved people. She loved the bright lights and the social world and she was a great pinnacle of it, no matter what people said about her. She was always invited out. She was the focal point of attention of any room she walked into. Everything stopped for a moment. And, of course, the scandals fed her a lot as well. But she had a lovely sense of humour and she was a very great lady.'

Tony Murkett confirmed that she went out most nights. 'There was always somebody collecting her.' Almost every night, right up to the very end of her time there. 'She was out six nights a week. She was rarely in during the evenings. And then at lunchtime she would just drink cold consommé.'

Margaret had gained considerable experience in 'working the system' of life and of the need to survive. She had the most beautiful clothes and shoes any woman could want and since she did not keep up with fashion trends, even old dresses looked classic, elegant and timeless. She would be seen in her 'uniforms' of neat black dresses adorned with her perfectly matched three strings of pearls, and perhaps a small diamond brooch. Nothing ostentatious. Her good taste was always unquestioned.

She accepted invitations to all the West End's opening nights, book launches, art exhibitions, birthday parties and celebratory dos. She loved going out and being seen. She was on every public relation company's list – she would go to the opening of an envelope.

She knew, however, that when she returned to her apartment she would have to face the ire of her personal maid, Edith Springett, who had by then been at the whisky. The earthy retainer was ten years older than Margaret. She was sprightly, bouncy and very active. But, like a cockney charlady, she would not suffer fools, and she certainly put Margaret in her place when the need arose, as Tony Murkett remembers: 'I was always called to Her Grace's apartment when there was trouble there. On this particular occasion I had to go up because she'd had an awful row with

Springett, who I found very amusing. I was called up by Her Grace, literally to boot Springett out. I refused to do this because it wasn't our business. Springett was *her* employee. It was the first time I'd been up to her apartment. I was a bit pensive because I had come from hotels without titled people. I knew her by reputation and I knew, at that time, she was quite important to the place. That got less and less as the years went by. As I went to the door, Springett held me back in the hallway. Her Grace used to come out of the drawing room into the hallway to see who was there, then beckon you in and retreat back. So you had a few seconds in the hallway always, when Springett would say what an old bitch she had been, and "She's so selfish," she's this, that and the other. Very, very derogatory. When I went into her drawing room she would be seated on her blue silk sofa, sipping cold consommé from this ten-ounce tumbler. Everybody thought it was a large tumbler of whisky, which was a bit unfair. In fact she never drank before six o'clock. And the first question Her Grace would ask would be about Springett: "Did she say anything to you in the hall? Was she rude about me? Did she make any rude signs?" and I'd say, "No, Your Grace, she's very charming about you." I'd never drop Springett in it, because she was a great source of information. But that day, there had been an almighty fight because Springett had called her very nasty names. I don't think there's any secret about that.'

However, Springett did not waste her abuse on Margaret when they were alone in the apartment. She waited until she had guests, and would refer to her employer, within earshot, in derogatory terms. This went on for a considerable time, until Margaret decided to complain to the management.

'Whenever there was an argument about domestic issues, Springett used to bring up all this dirt. She wasn't very good with words and I suppose it was her only defence mechanism. She'd just be very, very rude, and I suppose it worked because Her Grace was always offended by it.'

There were many such incidents. After Tony Murkett had been at the Grosvenor House for a couple of years, he was summoned to Margaret's presence. She told him that she felt that the Grosvenor House staff had become very rude. 'I thought it was just a mistake at first,' she started, 'but it's gone on for three days. It's obviously a scheme. It's obviously a plan, because everybody is calling me "Mrs Argyll".'

Tony suspected the ringleader was one of the hotel's valets, who was, if not a gossip, the 'oracle' of the staff's activities. He asked the man what he knew of the demotion. 'Well, Mr Murkett,' he said. 'Everybody's fed up. She expects us to bow and scrape to her. She wants us to run to her, but she's bloody rude. She thinks we're her servants, and we're not having any more. If she'd say thank you occasionally, or if she'd be nice to us, it would be different. So we all got together and decided to fix her. We decided to drop her title and call her Mrs Argyll so that she would feel offended.'

'And, of course, they got right to her heart. I sympathized with them, because it was the eighties and times were a little different. Naturally, we're terribly polite and gracious, but people won't get down on their knees any more. It's very difficult. So I went back to Her Grace and said that they found her awkward to deal with. I explained that they tried very hard to please her, but that, in return, she was unreasonable. I think it sank in because she replied, "OK. If that's the reason, I'll try to be nicer," which she was. And they immediately reverted to calling her Your Grace. But it was a real lesson to her, because while I had to be polite to her about it, I had to show a good deal of sympathy for my people who had tried terribly hard to please her.'

The staff had taught her a lesson in good manners, and Springett showed her disrespect in her own way, but dear old Springett had a fall, broke a leg and left Margaret's service. She died soon after.

Her next maid, however, led her a real dance. She ran up a telephone bill of over £8,000 on the private line and £3,000 on the hotel switchboard, and, naturally, couldn't afford to pay, so the burden fell on Margaret. But she was running into difficulties about paying her hotel bill and could not pay either. The police prosecuted the maid and she got a suspended sentence.

'I think she took Her Grace for a ride. I believe the Duchess was proved correct in court, and it was obvious that she abused the Duchess's trust. I remember many conversations about money and how she was trying to get money out of the Nassau trustees, but it never actually came. None of her family ever visited her. If they did, I didn't see them. She didn't speak well of any of them either.'

But there was hope on the horizon, and it promised a boost to Margaret's flagging fortune. She had always considered herself a star, and now, for the first time, her wish to be one in the true sense seemed about to come true.

An independent film production company, Park Productions, launched a project entitled *The Legacy* in 1987. They entered into an agreement with Margaret for her to appear as herself in the soap opera, the life story of one of the century's most talked-about characters. 'The production company spent a great deal of time with her,' Tony Murkett said, 'and I think they got her rather excited about something that didn't happen. She was very anxious to get money out of it and I think that contributed to her downhill climb. She must have been thoroughly disappointed over it, because she thought the whole thing, with her playing a major character, would materialize, right to the point when she was due to go on location.'

Park Productions had not reckoned with the tenacity of their prospective leading lady. When Margaret learnt that the production had been shelved, she marched into their office in central London and announced to the assembled company: 'I am sorry, gentlemen, I have come for my money.' She sat down and refused to leave until they produced the cheque for £10,000, the sum she was contracted to be paid on that particular day.

She was in her late seventies, and not the frail old lady they might have expected her to be. She held her ground, outstared them in stony silence, and they finally handed her the cheque. Her expectations had been greater. Her disappointment, bitter. Her last hope for the chance of real stardom and the prospect of making enough to keep abreast with her hotel bill had slipped through her fingers.

Although she felt the film company had let her down, none could have felt more disappointed by empty promises than the two young boys she had adopted. She had given them high hopes for their future and guaranteed them education and security until they were twenty-one. Jamie and Richard Gardner were dropped by her financially when they were sixteen. In an effort to make amends and to secure some kind of career for Jamie, she later pulled a few strings and arranged for Jamie to start at the Grosvenor House as a management trainee. 'I was slightly pushed into it,' he said. The work didn't suit him. He was young, the hours were long, and the work involved weekends and evenings. He had a wife and three young children by then, and saw little of them. Margaret seemed shocked when he finally gave up the job, and joined the fire service. Jamie's fireman's salary was £18,700 a year, on which he had to support his family. His brother, Richard, had done better: he worked in the City as an oil trader. But their hopes, built up since the ages of seven and nine, were dashed when Margaret dropped them.

Jamie said that he felt the reason for her stopping their education was because of the class structure: 'I think she thought there wasn't much point in boys like us going on to do A levels and university. She was rather naïve. I think she probably thought that I would end up as managing director of the Grosvenor House and would look after her there. She was the sort of woman who made everything stop when she walked into a restaurant,' he added with some admiration. 'She had an aura of power about her. I remember once she made such a fuss in one restaurant about the air-conditioning that in the end they laid on a car to take us home.'

He added that she did not set up a trust fund for them and that they were not remembered in her will.

Margaret's financial problems grew worse. She was given a gossip column in *Tatler* magazine with the by-line,

'Stepping out with Margaret Argyll', but her two-page jottings were reduced to a small corner of one within two years. She could not spell and her memory was short. By now her physical and mental faculties were failing.

Relatively speaking, most people have anxieties about their mortgages, rising prices, falling incomes and the cost of living. But she had the added problem concerning her physical incapacities in the dark twilight of her years. Lord Forte takes up the story.

He had built his magnificent empire since he left Italy as the young Charles Forte, the eldest of three children. When he was young, he joined his parents who had left Italy to start a business of ice-cream parlours in Scotland. He was later educated in Rome, and by the time he returned from Italy his family had moved to England. He opened his first milk-bar in Regent Street during the war years, and through his hard work and industry over the years was awarded, firstly, a knighthood and then made a member of the peerage. His sister, Anna Sanna, presides over the good taste and style of the grand interiors of the group's hotels in London, adding her own touch of flair and elegance for their guests' comfort. His dynamic son, Rocco, succeeded him as chairman of the board, and his eldest daughter, Olga, masterminded the interiors of the worldwide Forte hotel conglomerate. Forte's other four children, Marie-Louise, Gian-Carla, Irene and Portia, are all endowed with their father's business acumen, and with their mother Irene's deep devotion to family unity. Charles and Irene were married for over fifty years, and were a prime example of a partnership that personifies the sanctity of family life and values.

Lord and Lady Forte had met Margaret on several occasions. She had dined with them at their Belgravia home, and they found her charming and agreeable. 'She was a good-looking woman,' Lord Forte said at luncheon at one of his group's other hotels, the Waldorf in Aldwych. His wife had joined him to add her own praise for the woman she had found attractive and dignified. 'She was getting a large discount at the Grosvenor House,' Lord Forte volunteered. 'She had the apartment at a very, very reasonable rate. But she found it was expensive. Grosvenor House *is* expensive. But she couldn't afford it, and I couldn't afford to keep her. My job is to make money. My shareholders want me to produce profits. We are not a charitable organization. They want to see profits. Profits give them the dividends. She hadn't fallen too badly in arrears, but we couldn't afford to keep her there at our expense. At the expense of the shareholders. So the management had to tell her. She took it very well. We didn't have any bad feeling about it. She had her own personal worries, but we had to consider our own situation. There was no falling out. People living like that,' he added wisely, 'think it's the normal way of living. They can't live in any other way. She couldn't go and light the gas stove and make a meal. She'd never done it before, and she couldn't start it now. I, myself, can't mend anything. I try, though. I start and then I have to give up. I can't do anything that is artisan. I have never been conditioned to it, so I understand her perfectly. It's a pity when these people fall on bad times,' he said sympathetically. 'It can happen to the best of them. They are used to the best. Then they go around looking for people who can support them. She was very dignified and we did help her for a long time.'

She was never evicted – it just became obvious she could no longer afford to live there. At about this time her mind started to wander and she was deemed mentally incapable to continue to handle her affairs and made subject of a Court of Protection Order. Lord Forte, for his part, never pursued his debts, realizing she would not be able to pay the arrears. His staff went on treating Margaret with deference and courtesy until she left the hotel for good in 1990 through a side entrance to avoid the waiting press.

About this time her daughter, despite the friction that existed between them, had assumed responsibility for the day-to-day upkeep of her ailing mother. Her lifelong friend Lady d'Avigdor-Goldsmid came to her rescue and offered to sublet a self-contained flat in the same building that she herself lived in. She had also previously lent Margaret some money but, like Margaret's other creditors, she was unlikely to be repaid.

This was not designed to be a permanent arrangement, though. Because of Margaret's frail health it was essential for her to have a nurse and a maid in attendance at all times. The arrangement was not a success. She therefore left soon after for St George's Nursing Home in Pimlico. There, under the care of the matron, Elizabeth McManus, and her dedicated staff, Margaret stayed in one room, with a shared bathroom situated up the corridor. Privation was alien to her. Nearing eighty, she was reduced to something approaching discomfort for the first time in her life. Close friends visited her from time to time, and she would sit alone in the entrance hall, watching the visitors on their way to her aged friends. They recognized the faded beauty that was hers, but passed like ghosts in the night. By now little registered with Margaret. They came and they left. This was her only activity. When some time later a far more luxurious self-contained flat in a more isolated wing became available, and was offered by the nursing home at no extra cost, this was declined as it would deny Margaret her only pleasure of watching the world go by. When they had gone, she was alone in her solitary room. 'It was so awful that they put her in a home,' Moira Lister said sadly. 'I went to see her two or three times. She said, "You know where they've put me, don't you? They've put me in the basement of my home in

Grosvenor Square." And I was sitting with her there, on the fourth floor of the nursing home. There were bars on the windows and she was seated thinking she was behind the bars of her basement in Mayfair. And she said, "Of course, I'm leaving soon. I'm getting out." She always thought she was getting out. When I walked in there, I saw this huge picture of her father on the wall and two pictures of her children. There were no pictures of the grandchildren, only these two of Frances aged about six months old and Brian when he was two years old. No modern pictures. And I thought, You're not getting out of here.'

Moira Lister also dispelled the rumour that Margaret had been drinking heavily – or drinking at all. Press reports had indicated that she had been consuming at least a bottle of whisky a day. Tony Murkett confirmed that neither he nor his staff at the Grosvenor House had ever seen her drinking.

'When they brought her lunch,' Moira Lister continued, 'there was never a glass of wine. She could have had it if she wanted it. But she never had anything to drink. I don't think she was ever a drinker. She would never have had that skin or that face if she were a drinker. And certainly not whisky, which is very harsh. It's a man's drink.'

Margaret remained autocratic to the end. 'When I was there,' Moira Lister continued, 'they brought this lunch to her on a tray at twelve o'clock, and she said, "What time is it?" The nurse said, "It's twelve o'clock." And she said, "Take this lunch away. Proper people don't lunch at twelve o'clock. Only servants eat at twelve o'clock. Take it away and bring it back at one o'clock." Of course, they didn't move it. They left it there and it just got colder and colder, and finally when she was hungry, she ate it. That place was so unlike her. It was a tiny little room. And it was £750 a week. Loelia, Duchess of Westminster, died there a few months later and that's where they put Evelyn Laye as well.'

But who paid the bill? In fact it was her daughter, Frances.

In spite of Margaret's failing health, she still never let slip her personal appearance. Pride, vanity, self-regard and dignity had never eluded her.

'At the nursing home,' Moira Lister continued, 'she had one of those trays that you put over your knee. All her make-up was on that, beautifully and neatly laid out; her nail varnish, her lipstick; and right until the end she made her face up, and had someone come in to do her hair. And they must have taken a lot of her beautiful clothes to her there because every day she was beautifully dressed. Beautiful stockings and shoes, and she always wore her pearls. She still looked wonderful. She really did. She was a great lady.'

Margaret died in her sleep in the early hours of the morning on Monday 26 July 1993. She had climbed out of bed to visit the bathroom and fell over. She was helped back into bed by the nursing staff but shortly after midnight she called out for her dog. Then there was a heavy thud. The nurses rushed into her room and found her lying on the floor beside the armchair.

After cleansing blood away from her eye, they helped her back into bed. She seemed to fall asleep, but she was, in fact, unconscious. She had suffered a serious head injury and had also broken her neck when she fell against the armchair. Her poodle, Louis, sat at her bedside waiting for his mistress to wake up in the morning. He waited in vain.

Margaret had become pitifully frail. Almost all the parts of her body were just wearing out. In the last four years of her life she suffered six strokes. In her last months she suffered severe loss of memory, incontinence, thyroid failure and unsteadiness.

At 1.20 a.m. a Roman Catholic priest gave her the last rites and thirty-five minutes later she was dead.

Louis, her pet poodle, had become the mascot of the nursing home and upon Margaret's death the Matron offered to keep him. He was loved by all the patients, particularly Evelyn Laye, and often went into Margaret's old room to cry for his mistress.

Eight days after her death, Margaret departed for her final resting place on Tuesday 3 August 1993. Her funeral mass was attended by two hundred mourners at the

Church of the Immaculate Conception in Farm Street, Mayfair. The congregation included her son and daughter, the Duke of Rutland and two of her grandchildren, Lady Theresa Manners and Lord Edward Manners, together with her most devoted friends.

Margaret had broken several hearts and destroyed many reputations throughout her lifelong quest for superiority over her peers. After her dance to the great bands and orchestras that brought flair to her years of disgrace, the solo mouth-organ of Larry Adler at the service echoed the solitary end of Margaret, Duchess of Argyll's play with life.

Her burial was a solitary affair attended only by her family and her lawyer. Before the coffin could be taken out of the hearse two camera crews were asked to leave by her son. Those present were determined that in death, unlike in life, hers would be a totally private departure. She was laid to rest next to her first husband – perhaps the only man she had ever loved.

She had known everybody, been everywhere, had every material advantage, been bestowed with legendary good looks.

Never had so much fortune been used to achieve so little.